VISIONS AND REVISIONS

A BOOK OF LITERARY DEVOTIONS

BY

JOHN COWPER POWYS

Staff Lecturer on Literature for Oxford University Extension Delegacy. Education Department Free City of Hamburg. Verein fuer Neuere Philologie, Dresden and Leipzig. University Lecturers' Association, New York

Ham.—Would not this, sir, and a forest of feathers—if the rest of my fortunes turn Turk with me—with two Provincial roses on my raz'd shoes, get me a fellowship in a cry of players, sir?
Hor.—Half a share.

ESSAY INDEX IN REPRINT

GREAT NECK, NEW YORK

FIRST PUBLISHED 1915
REPRINTED 1978

INTERNATIONAL STANDARD BOOK NUMBER 0-8486-3025-4

LIBRARY OF CONGRESS CATALOG NUMBER
78-58263

PRINTED IN THE UNITED STATES OF AMERICA

To Those who love
  Without understanding;
To Those who understand
  Without loving;
  And to Those
Who, neither loving or understanding,
  Are the Cause
  Why Books are written.

CONTENTS

Preface	9
Rabelais	25
Dante	35
Shakespeare	55
El Greco	75
Milton	87
Charles Lamb	105
Dickens	119
Goethe	135
Matthew Arnold	153
Shelley	169
Keats	183
Nietzsche	197
Thomas Hardy	213
Walter Pater	227
Dostoievsky	241
Edgar Allen Poe	263
Walt Whitman	281
Conclusion	293

PREFACE

HAT I aim at in this book is little more than to give complete reflection to those great figures in Literature which have so long obsessed me. This poor reflection of them passes, as they pass, image by image, eidolon by eidolon, in the flowing stream of my own consciousness.

Most books of critical essays take upon themselves, in unpardonable effrontery, to weigh and judge, from their own petty suburban pedestal, the great Shadows they review. It is an insolence! How should Professor This, or Doctor That, whose furthest experiences of "dangerous living" have been squalid philanderings with their neighbours' wives, bring an Ethical Synthesis to bear that shall put Shakespeare and Hardy, Milton and Rabelais, into appropriate niches?

Every critic has a right to his own Aesthetic Principles, to his own Ethical Convictions; but when it comes to applying these, in tiresome, pedantic agitation, to Edgar Allen

Poe and Charles Lamb, we must beg leave to cry off! What we want is not the formulating of new Critical Standards, and the dragging in of the great masters before our last miserable Theory of Art. What we want is an honest, downright and quite *personal* articulation, as to how these great things in literature really hit us when they find us for the moment natural and off our guard—when they find us as men and women, and not as ethical gramaphones.

My own object in these sketches is not to convert the reader to whatever "opinions" I may have formulated in the course of my spiritual adventures; it is to divest myself of such "opinions," and in pure, passionate humility to give myself up, absolutely and completely, to the various visions and temperaments of these great dead artists.

There is an absurd notion going about, among those half-educated people who frequent Ethical Platforms, that Literary Criticism must be "constructive." O that word "constructive"! How, in the name of the mystery of genius, can criticism be anything else than an idolatry, a worship, a metamorphosis, a love affair! The pathetic mistake these people make is to fancy that the great artists only lived and wrote in order to buttress up such poor wretches as these are upon the particular little, thin, cardboard platform

PREFACE

which is at present their moral security and refuge.

No one has a right to be a critic whose mind cannot, with Protean receptivity, take first one form and then another, as the great Spells, one by one, are thrown and withdrawn.

Who wants to know what Professor So-and-so's view of Life may be? We want to use Professor So-and-so as a Mirror, as a Medium, as a Go-Between, as a Sensitive Plate, so that we may once more get the thrill of contact with this or that dead Spirit. He must keep his temperament, our Critic; his peculiar angle of receptivity, his capacity for personal reaction. But it is the reaction of his own natural nerves that we require, not the pallid, second-hand reaction of his tedious, formulated opinions. Why cannot he see that, as a natural man, physiologically, nervously, temperamentally, pathologically *different* from other men, he is an interesting spectacle, as he comes under the influence first of one great artist and then another, while as a silly, little, preaching school-master, he is only a blot upon the world-mirror!

It is thus that I, moi qui vous parle, claim my humble and modest role. If, in my reaction from Rabelais, for instance, I find myself responding to his huge laughter at "love" and other things, and a moment later, in my reaction from Thomas Hardy, feeling as if "love" and the rest were the only important matters in the Universe; this psychological variability, itself of interest as a curious human phenomenon, has made it possible to get the "reflections," each absolute in its way, of the two great artists as they advance and recede.

If I had tried to dilute and prune and "correct" the one, so as to make it "fit in" with the other, in some stiff, ethical theory of my own, where would be the interest for the reader? Besides, who am I to "improve" upon Rabelais?

It is because so many of us are so limited in our capacity for "variable reaction" that there are so few good critics. But we are all, I think, more multiple-souled than we care to admit. It is our foolish pride of consistency, our absurd desire to be "constructive," that makes us so dull. A critic need not necessarily approach the world from the "pluralistic" angle; but there must be something of such "pluralism" in his natural temper, or the writers he can respond to will be very few!

Let it be quite plainly understood. It is impossible to respond to a great genius halfway. It is a case of all or nothing. If you lack the courage, or the variability, to *go all the way* with very different masters, and to let your constructive consistency take care of itself, you may become, perhaps, an admirable moralist;

PREFACE

you will never be a clairvoyant critic. All this having been admitted, it still remains that one has a right to draw out from the great writers one loves certain universal aesthetic tests, with which to discriminate between modern productions.

But even such tests are personal and relative. They are not to be foisted on one's readers as anything "ex cathedra." One such test is the test of what has been called "the grand style"—that grand style against which, as Arnold says, the peculiar vulgarity of our race beats in vain! I do not suppose I shall be accused of perverting my devotion to the "grand style" into an academic "narrow way," through which I would force every writer I approach. Some most winning and irresistible artists never come near it.

And yet—what a thing it is! And with what relief do we return to it, after the "wallowings" and "rhapsodies," the agitations and prostitutions, of those who have it not!

It is—one must recognize that—the thing, and the only thing, that, in the long run, *appeals*. It is because of the absence of it that one can read so few modern writers *twice!* They have flexibility, originality, cleverness, insight—but they lack *distinction*—they fatally lack distinction.

And what are the elements, the qualities, that go to make up this "grand style"?

VISIONS AND REVISIONS

Let me first approach the matter negatively. There are certain things that *cannot*—because of something essentially ephemeral in them—be dealt with in the grand style.

Such are, for instance, our modern controversies about the problem of Sex. We may be Feminists or Anti-Feminists—what you will—and we may be able to throw interesting light on these complicated relations, but we cannot write of them, either in prose or poetry, in the grand style, because the whole discussion is ephemeral; because, with all its gravity, it is irrelevant to the things that ultimately matter!

Such, to take another example, are our elaborate arguments about the interpretation, ethical or otherwise, of Christian Doctrine. We can be very entertaining, very moral, very eloquent, very subtle, in this particular sphere; but we cannot deal with it in the "great style," because the permanent issues that really count lie out of reach of such discussion and remain unaffected by it.

Let me make myself quite clear. Hector and Andromache can talk to one another of their love, of their eternal parting, of their child, and they can do this in the great style; but if they fell into dispute over the particular sex conventions that existed in their age, they might be attractive still, but they would not be uttering words in the "great style."

PREFACE

Matthew Arnold may argue eloquently about the true modernistic interpretation of the word "Elohim," and very cleverly and wittily give his reasons for translating it "the Eternal" or "the Shining One"; but into what a different atmosphere we are immediately transported when, in the midst of such discussion, the actual words of the Psalmist return to our mind: "My soul is athirst for God—yea! even for the living God! When shall I come to appear before the presence of God?"

The test is always that of Permanence, and of immemorial human association. It is, at bottom, nothing but human association that makes the great style what it is. Things that have, for centuries upon centuries, been associated with human pleasures, human sorrows, and the great recurrent dramatic moments of our lives, can be expressed in this style; and only such things. The great style is a sort of organic, self-evolving work of art, to which the innumerable units of the great human family have all put their hands. That is why so large a portion of what is written in the great style is anonymous—like Homer and much of the Bible and certain old ballads and songs. It is for this reason that Walter Pater is right when he says that the important thing in Religion is the Ceremony, the Litany, the Ritual, the Liturgical Chants, and not the Creeds or the Commandments, or discussion upon Creed or Commandment. Creeds change, Morality changes, Mysticism changes, Philosophy changes—but the Word of our God—the Word of Humanity—in gesture, in ritual, in the heart's natural crying—abideth forever!

Why do the eloquent arguments of an ethical orator, explaining to us our social duties, go a certain way and never go further, whereas we have only to hear that long-drawn *Vox Humana,* old as the world—older certainly than any creed—"Santa Maria, Mater Dei, ora pro nobis peccatoribus, nunc et in hora mortis nostræ"—and we are struck, disarmed, pierced to the marrow, smitten to the bone, shot through, "Tutto tremente?" Because arguments and reasoning; because morality and logic, are not of the nature of the "great style," while the cry—"save us from eternal death!"—addressed by the passion and remorse and despair of our human heart to the unhearing Universe, takes that great form as naturally as a man breathes.

Why, of all the religious books in the world, have "the Psalms of David," whether in Hebrew or Latin or English, touched men's souls and melted and consoled them? They are not philosophical. They are not logical. They are not argumentative. They are not moral. And yet they break our hearts with their beauty and their appeal!

It is the same with certain well-known

PREFACE

words. Is it understood, for instance, why the word "Sword" is always poetical and in "the grand style," while the word "Zeppelin" or "Submarine" or "Gatling gun" or "Howitzer" can only be introduced by Free Versifiers, who let the "grand style" go to the Devil? The word "Sword,' like the word "Plough," has gathered about it the human associations of innumerable centuries, and it is impossible to utter it without feeling something of their pressure and their strain. The very existence of the "grand style" is a protest against any false views of "progress" and "evolution." Man may alleviate his lot in a thousand directions; he may build up one Utopia after another; but the grand style will still remain; will remain as the ultimate expression of those aspects of his life that *cannot change*—while he remains Man.

If there is any unity in these essays, it will be found in a blurred and stammered attempt to indicate how far it may be possible, in spite of the limitations of our ordinary nature, to live in the light of the "grand style." I do not mean that we—the far-off worshippers of these great ones—can live *as they thought and felt.* But I mean that we can live in the atmosphere, the temper, the mood, the attitude towards things, which "the grand style" they use evokes and sustains.

I want to make this clear. There are a certain number of solitary spirits moving among us who have a way of troubling us by their aloofness from our controversies, our disputes, our arguments, our "great problems." We call them Epicures, Pagans, Heathen, Egoists, Hedonists, and Virtuosos. And yet not one of these words exactly fits them. What they are really doing is living in the atmosphere and the temper of "the grand style"—and that is why they are so irritating and provocative! To them the most important thing in the world is to realize to the fullest limit of their consciousness what it means to be born a Man. The actual drama of our mortal existence, reduced to the simplest terms, is enough to occupy their consciousness and their passion. In this sphere—in the sphere of the "inevitable things" of human life—everything becomes to them a sacrament. Not a symbol—be it noted—but a Sacrament! The food they eat; the wine they drink; their waking and sleeping; the hesitancies and reluctances of their devotions; the swift anger of their recoils and retreats; their long loyalties; their savage reversions; their sudden "lashings out"; their hate and their love and their affection; the simplicities of these everlasting moods are in all of us—become, every one of them, matters of sacramental efficiency. To regard each day, as it dawns, as a "last day," and to make of its sunrise, of its noon, of its sun-setting, a rhythmic antiphony to the eternal gods—this is to live in the spirit of the "grand style." It has nothing to do with "right" or "wrong." Saints may practise it, and sometimes do. Sinners often practise it. The whole thing consists in growing vividly conscious of those moods and events which are permanent and human, as compared with those other moods and events which are transitory and unimportant.

When a man or woman experiences desire, lust, hate, jealousy, devotion, admiration, passion, they are victims of the eternal forces, that can speak, if they will, in "the great style." When a man or woman "argues" or "explains" or "moralizes" or "preaches," they are the victims of accidental dust-storms, which rise from futility and return to vanity. That is why Rhetoric, as Rhetoric, can never be in the great style. That is why certain great revolutionary Anarchists, those who have the genius to express in words their heroic defiance of "the something rotten in Denmark," move us more, and assume a grander outline, than the equally admirable, and possibly more practical, arguments of the Scientific Socialists. It is the eternal appeal we want, to what is basic and primitive and undying in our tempestuous human nature!

The grand style announces and commands. It weeps and it pleads. It utters oracles and it wrestles with angels. It never apologises; it never rationalizes; and it never explains. That is why the great ineffable passages in the supreme masters take us by the throat and strike us dumb. Deep calls unto Deep in them, and our heart listens and is silent. To "do good scientific thinking" in the cause of humanity has its well-earned reward; but the gods "throw incense" on a different temper. The "fine issues" that reach them, in their remoteness and their disdain, are the "fine issues" of an antagonist worthy of their own swift wrath, their own swift vengeance, and their own swift love.

The ultimate drama of the world, a drama never-ending, lies between the children of Zeus and the children of Prometheus; between the hosts of Jehovah and the Sons of the Morning. God and Lucifer still divide the Stage, and in Homer, Shakespeare, Dante, Milton, and Goethe the great style is never more the great style than when it brings these eternal Antagonists face to face, and compels them to cross swords. What matter if, in reality, they have their kingdoms in the heart of man rather than the Empyrean or Tartarus? The heart of man, in its unchangeable character, must ever remain the true Coliseum of the world, where the only interesting, the only dramatic, the only beautiful, the only classical things are born and turned into music!

PREFACE

Beauty! That is what we all, even the grossest of us, in our heart of hearts is seeking. Lust seeks it; Love creates it, the miracle of Faith finds it—but nothing less, neither truth or wisdom or morality or knowledge, neither progress or reaction, can quench the thirst we feel.

RABELAIS

RABELAIS

HERE are certain great writers who make their critics feel even as children, who picking up stray wreckage and broken shells from the edge of the sea waves, return home to show their companions "what the sea is like."

The huge suggestiveness of this tremendous spirit is not easy to communicate in the space of a little essay.

But something can be done, if it only take the form of modest "advice to the reader."

Is it a pity, one asks oneself, or is it a profound advantage, that enjoyment of Rabelais should be so limited? At least there are no false versions to demolish here—no idealizations to unmask.

The reading of Rabelais is not easy to everyone, and perhaps to those for whom it is least easy, he would be most medicinal. What in this mad world, do we lack, my dear friends? Is it possibly *courage?* Well, Rabelais is, of all writers, the one best able to give us that courage. If only we had courage, how the great tides of existence might sweep us along—and we not whine or wince at all!

VISIONS AND REVISIONS

To read Rabelais is to gather, as if from the earth-gods, spirit to endure anything. Naturally he uses wine, and every kind of wanton liquor, to serve as symbols of the intoxication he would produce. For we must be "rendered drunk" to swallow Life at this rate—to swallow it as the gods swallow it. We must be drunk but not mad. For in the spiritual drunkenness that Rabelais produces there is not the remotest touch of insanity. He is the sanest of all the great writers; perhaps the only sane one. What he has the power of communicating to us is a renewal of that *physiological energy,* which alone makes it possible to enjoy this monstrous world. Other writers interpret things, or warn us against things. Rabelais takes us by the hand, shows us the cup of life, deep as eternity, and bids us drink and be satisfied. What else could he use, if not *wine,* as a symbol for such quenching of such thirst. And after wine, sex. There is no other who treats sex as Rabelais does; who treats it so completely as it *ought* to be treated!

Walt Whitman is too obsessed by it; too grave over it—Rabelais enjoys it, fools with it, plunges into it, wallows in it; and then, with multitudinous laughter, shakes himself free, and bids it go to the Devil!

The world will have to come to this, sooner or later—to the confusion of the vicious—and the virtuous!

RABELAIS

The virtuous and the vicious play indeed into each others hands; and neither of them love laughter. Sexual dalliance is either too serious a matter to be mocked by satyr-laughter; or it is too sad and deplorable to be laughed at at all. In a few hundred years, surely, the human race will recognize its absolute right to make mock at the grotesque elements in the sex comedy, and such laughter will clear the air of much "virtue" and much "vice."

Wine is his first symbol of the large, sane, generous mood he bequeaths to us—the focusing of the poetry of life, and the glow and daring of it, and its eternal youthfulness.

But it is more than a symbol—it is a sacrament and an initiation. It is the sap that rises in the world's recurrent spring. It is the ichor, the quintessence of the creative mystery. It is the blood of the sons of the morning. It is the dew upon the paradisic fields. It is the red-rose light, upon the feet of those who dance upon graves. Wine is a sign to us how there is required a certain generous and sane intoxication, a certain large and equable friendliness in dealing with people and things and ideas. It is a sign that the earth calls aloud for the passionate dreamer. It is a sign that the truth of truth is not in labor and sorrow, but in joy and happiness. It is a sign that gods and men have a right to satisfy their hearts desire, with joy and pleasure and splendid freedom.

VISIONS AND REVISIONS

And just as he uses wine, so he uses meat. Bread that strengtheneth man's heart (and bologna-sausages, gammons of bacon, or what you will, else) this also is a symbol and a sacrament. And it is indeed more, for one must remember that Rabelais was a great doctor of medicine, as well as of Utopian Theology—and the stomach, with the wise indulgence thereof, is the final master of all arts! Let it be understood that in Rabelais sex is treated with the same reverence, and the same humor, as meat and wine. Why not? Is not the body of man the temple of the Holy Ghost? Is it not sacrosanct and holy within and without; and yet, at the same time, is it not a huge and palpable absurdity?

Those who suffer most from Rabelais' manner of treating sex are the incurably vicious. The really evil libidinous people, that is to say the spiteful, the mean, the base and inhuman, fly from his presence, and for the obvious reason that he makes sex-pleasure so generous, so gay, so natural, so legitimate, that their dark morbid perverted natures can get no more joy out of it. Their lust, their lechery, is a cold dead Saurian thing, a thing with the gravity of a slow-worm—and when this great laughing and generous sage comes forth into the sunshine with his noble companies of amorous and happy people, these Shadow-lovers, these Leut-lovers, these Fleshly Sentimentalists, writhe in shame, and seek refuge in a deeper darkness. How strained and inhuman, too; and one might add, how mad and irrelevant— that high, cold, disdainful translunar scorn with which the "moral-immoralism" of Nietzsche scourges our poor flesh and blood. One turns with relief to Zarathustra after associating with pious people. But, after Rabelais, even that terrific psychologist seems contorted and *thin*.

For after all it is generosity that we cry out for. Courage without generosity hugs its knees in Hell.

From the noble pleasures of meat and drink and sex, thus generously treated; we must turn to another aspect of Rabelais' work—his predilection for excrement. This also, though few would admit it, is a symbolic secret. This also is a path of initiation. In this peculiarity Rabelais is completely alone among the writers of the earth. Others have, for various reasons, dabbled in this sort of thing—but none have ever piled it up—manure-heap upon manure-heap, until the animal refuse of the whole earth seems to reek to the stars! There is not the slightest reason to regret this thing or to expurgate it. Rabelais is not Rabelais, just as life is not life, without it.

It is indeed the way of "salvation" for certain neurotic natures. Has that been properly understood? There are people who suffer frightfully—and they are often rare natures, too, though they are sometimes very vicious—from their loathing of the excremental side of life. Swift was one of these. The "disgusting" in his writing is a pathological form, not at all unusual, of such a loathing. But Rabelais is no Dean Swift—nor is there the remotest resemblance between them. Rabelais may really save us from our loathing by the huge all-embracing friendliness of his sense of humor.

There are certain people, no doubt, who would prefer the grave enthusiasm of Whitman in regard to this matter to the freer Rabelaisian touch. I cannot say that my personal experience agrees with this view.

I have found both great men invaluable; but I think as far as dealing with the Cloaca Maxima side of things is concerned, Rabelais has been the braver in inspiration. In these little matters one can only say, "some are born Rabelaisian, and some require to have Rabelais thrust upon them!"

Surely it is wisdom, in us terrestial mortals, to make what imaginative use we can of *every phase* of our earthly condition?

Imagination has a right to play with everything that exists; and humor has a right to laugh at everything that exists. Everything in life is sacred and everything is a huge jest.

It is the association of this excremental

aspect of life, with those high sacraments of meat and drink and sex, which some find so hard to endure. Be not afraid my little ones! The great and humorous gods have arranged for this also; and have seen to it that no brave, generous, amorous "sunburnt" emotion shall ever be hurt by such associations! If a person *is* hurt by them, that is only an indication that they are in grievous need of the wholesome purgative medicine of the great doctor! When one comes to speak of the actual contents of these books criticism itself must borrow Gargantua's mouth.

What characters! The three great royal giants, Graugousier, Gargantua and Pantagruel—have there ever been such kings? And the noble servants of such noble masters! The whole atmosphere is so large, so genial, so courteous, so sweet-tempered, so entirely what the life of man upon earth should be.

Even the military exploits of Friar John, even the knavish tricks of Panurge, cannot spoil our tenderness for these dear bully-boys, these mellow and magnanimous rogues! Certain paragraphs in Rabelais recur to one's mind daily. That laudation of Socrates at the beginning, and the description of the "little boxes called *Sileni*" that outside have so grotesque an adornment, but within are full of ambergris and myrrh and all manner of precious odours.

And the picture of the banquet "when they

fell to the chat of the afternoon's collation and began great goblets to ring, great bowls to ting, great gammons to trot; pour me out the fair Greek wine, the extravagant wine, the good wine, Lacrima Christi, supernaculum!" And, above all, the most holy Abbey of Thelema, over the gate of which was written the words that are never far from the hearts of wise Utopian Christians, the profound words, the philosophical words, the most shrewd Cabalistic words, and the words that "lovers" alone can understand—"Fay que ce Vouldray!" Do as Thou Wilt!

Little they know of Rabelais who call him a lewd buffoon—the profanest of mountebanks. He was one of those rare spirits that redeem humanity. To open his book—though the steam of the grossness of it rises to Heaven—is to touch the divine fingers—the fingers that heal the world.

How that "style" of his, that great oceanic avalanche of learning and piety and obscenity and gigantic merriment, smells of the honest earth!

How, with all his huge scholarship, he loves to depend for his richest, most human effects, upon his own peasant-people of Touraine! The proverbs of the country-side, the wisdom of tavern-wit, the shrewdness and fantasy of old wives tales, the sly earthly humors of farmers and vine-tenders and goat-herds and goose-girls. These are things out of which he distils his vision, his oracles, his courage.

There is also—who could help observing it?—a certain large and patriarchal homeliness—a kind of royal domesticity—about much that he writes. Those touches, as when Gargantua, his little dog in advance, enters the dining hall, when they are discussing Panurge's marriage, and they all rise to do him honor; as when Gargantua bids Pantagruel farewell and gives him a benediction so wise and tender; remain in the mind like certain passages in the Bible. These are the things that æsthetic fools "with varnished faces" easily overlook and misunderstand; but good simple fellows—"honest cods" as Rabelais would say—are struck to the heart by them. How proud the man might be, who in the turmoil of this troublesome world and beneath the mystery of "le grand Penetre" could answer to the ultimate question, "I am a Christian of the faith of Rabelais!"

Such a one, under the spell of such a master, might indeed be able to comfort the sick and sorry, and to whisper in their ears that cosmic secret—"Bon Espoir y gist au fond!" "Good Hope lies at the Bottom!" "Good Hope" for all; for the best and the worst—for the whole miserable welter of this chaotic farce!

Therefore, "with angels and archangels" let us bow our heads and hold our tongues. Those who fancy Rabelais to be lacking in the kind of religious feeling that great souls respect, let them read that passage in the voyage of Pantagruel that speaks of the Death of Pan. Various accounts are given; various explanations made; of the great cry, that the sailors, "coming from Paloda," heard over land and sea. At the last Pantagruel himself speaks; and he tells them that to him it refers to nothing less than the death of Him whom the Scribes and Pharisees and Priests of Jerusalem slew. "And well is He called Pan, which in the Greek means "All"; for in Him is all we are or have or hope." And having said this he fell into silence, and "tears large as ostrich-eggs rolled down his cheeks."

To all who read Rabelais and love him, one can offer no better wish than that the mystic wine of his Holy Bottle may fulfil their heart's desire. Happy, indeed, those who are not "unwillingly drawn" by the "Fate" we all must follow! "Go now, my friends," says the strange Priestess, "and may that Circle whose Centre is everywhere and its Circumference nowhere, keep you in His Almighty protection!"

DANTE

DANTE

HE history of Dante's personal and literary appeal would be an extremely interesting one. No great writer has managed to excite more opposite emotions.

One thing may be especially noted as significant: Women have always been more attracted to him than men. He is in a peculiar sense the Woman's great poet. There is a type of masculine genius which has always opposed him. Goethe cared little for him; Voltaire laughed at him; Nietzsche called him "an hyæna poetizing among the tombs."

The truth is, women love Dante for the precise reason that these men hate him. He makes sex the centre of everything. One need not be deceived by the fact that Dante worships "purity," while Voltaire, Goethe and Nietzsche are little concerned with it. This very laudation of continence is itself an emphasis upon sex. These others would play with amorous propensities; trifle with them in their life, in their art, in their philosophy; and then, that dangerous plaything laid aside would, as Machiavel puts it, "assume suitable attire, and return to the company of their equals—the great sages of antiquity."

Now it is quite clear that this pagan attitude towards sex, this tendency to enjoy it in its place and leave it there, is one that, more than anything else, is irritating to women. If, as a German thinker says, every woman is a courtezan or a mother, it is obvious that the artists and thinkers who refuse alike the beguilements of the one and the ironic tenderness of the other, are not people to be "loved." Dante refuses neither; and he has, further, that peculiar mixture of harsh strength and touching weakness, which is so especially appealing to women. They are reluctantly overcome—not without pleasure— by his fierce authority; and they can play the "little mother" to his weakness. The maternal instinct is as ironical as it is tender. It smiles at the high ideals or the eccentric child it pets, but it would not have him different. What a woman does not like, whether she is mother or courtezan, is that other kind of irony, the irony of the philosopher, which undermines both her maternal feeling and her passionate caresses.

Women, too, even quite good women, have the stress of the sexual difference constantly before them. Indeed it may be said that the class of women who are least sex-conscious are those who have habitually to sell themselves. It all matters so little then!

DANTE

How fiercely is the interest of the most virtuous aroused, when any question of a love affair is rumored. In this sense every woman is a born "go-between." Sex is not with them a thing apart, an exciting volcanic thing, liable to mad outbursts, to weird perversions, but often completely forgotten. It is never completely forgotten. It is diffused. It is everywhere. It lurks in a thousand innocent gestures and intimations. The savage purity of an Artemis is no real exception. Sex is a thing too pressing to be dallied with. It is all or nothing.

One cannot play with fire. When we make observations of this kind we do not derogate from the charm or dignity of women. It is no aspersion upon them. They did not ask to have it so. It is so.

Domestic life as the European nations have evolved it is a queer compromise. Its restraints weigh heavily, in alternate discord, upon both sexes.

Masculine depravity rebels against it, and the whole modern feministic movement shakes it to the base. It remains to be seen whether Nature will admit of any satisfactory readjustment.

Certainly, as far as overt acts are concerned, women are far "purer" than men. It is only when we leave the sphere of outward acts and enter the sphere of cerebral undercurrents, that all this is changed. There the Biblical story finds its proof, and the daughters of Eve revert to their mother. This is the secret of that mania for the personal which characterizes women's conversation. She can say fine things and do fine work; but both in her wit and her art, one is conscious of a mind that has voluptuously welcomed, or vindictively repulsed, the approach of a particular invasion; never of a mind that, in its abstract love for the beautiful, cannot even remember how it came to give birth to such thoughts!

It is the close psychological association between the emotion of religion and the emotion of sex which has always made women more religious than men.

This is perhaps only to say that women are nearer the secret of the universe than men. It may well be so. Man's rationalizing tendency to divorce his intelligence from his intuition—may not be the precise key which opens those magic doors! *Sanctity* itself—that most exquisite flower of the art of character—is a profoundly feminine thing. The most saintly saints, that is to say those who wear the indescribable distinction of their Master, are always possessed of a certain feminine quality.

Sanctity is woman's ideal—morality is man's. The one is based upon passion, and by means of love lifts us above law. The other is based upon vice and the recoil from vice; and has no horizons of any sort.

DANTE

That is why the countries where the imagination is profoundly feminine like Russia and France have sanctity as their ideal. Whereas England has its Puritan morality, and Germany its scientific efficiency. These latter races ought to sit at Dante's feet, to learn the secret of the "Beatific Vision" that is as far beyond morality as it is outside science. There are, it is true, certain moments when the Italian poet leads us up into the cold rarified air of that "Intellectual Love of God" which leaves sex, as it leaves other human feelings, infinitely behind. But this Spinozistic mood is not the natural climate of his soul. He is always ready to revert, always anxious to "drag Beatrice in." Wagner's "Parsifal" is perhaps the most flagrant example of this ambiguous association between religion and sex. The sentimental blasphemy of that feet-washing scene is an evidence of the depths of sexual morbidity into which this voluptuous religion of pity can lead us. O that figure in the white nightgown, blessing his reformed harlot!

It is a pity Wagner ever touched the Celtic Legend—German sentimentality and Celtic romance need a Heine to deal with them!

It is indeed a difficult task to write of the relations between romantic love and devotional religion and to do it in the grand style. That is where Dante is so supremely great. And that is why, for all his greatness, his influence upon modern art has been so morbid and evil. The odious sensuality of the so-called "Pre-Raphaelite School"—a sensuality drenched with holy water and perfumed with incense—has a smell of corruption about it that ought never to be associated with Dante's name.

The worst of modern poets, the most affected and the most meticulous, are all anxious to seal themselves of the tribe of Dante. But they are no more like that divine poet than the flies that feed on a dead Cæsar are like the hero they cause to stink!

Our brave Oscar understood him. Some of the most exquisite passages in "Intentions" refer to his poetry. Was the "Divine Comedy" too clear-cut and trenchant for Walter Pater? It is strange how Dante has been left to second-rate interpreters! His illustrators, too! O these sentimentalists, with their Beatrices crossing the Ponte Vecchio, and their sad youths looking on! All this is an insult—a sacrilege—to the proudest, most aristocratic spirit who ever dwelt on earth! Why did not Aubrey Beardsley stop that beautiful boy on the threshold? He who was the model of his "Ave atque vale!" might have well served for Casella, singing among the cold reeds, in the white dawn.

For there are scenes in Dante which have the strange, remote, perverted, *archaic* loveliness of certain figures on the walls of Egyptian temples or on the earliest Greek vases. Here the real artist in him forgets God and Beatrice and the whole hierarchy of the saints. And it is because of things of this kind that many curious people are found to be his worshipers who will never themselves pass forth "to rebehold the stars." They are unwise who find Dante so bitter and theological, so Platonic and devoted, that they cannot open his books. They little know what ambiguous planets, what dark heathen meteors move on the fringe of his great star-lit road. His Earthly Lady, as well as his Heavenly Lady, may have the moon beneath her feet.

But neither of them know, as does their worshiper and lover, *what lies on the other side of the moon.*

What Dante leaves to us as his ultimate gift is his pride and his humility. The one answers the other. And both put us to shame. He, alone of great artists, holds in his hand the true sword of the Spirit for the dividing asunder of men and things. There is no necessity to lay all the stress upon the division between the Lower and the Higher Love, between Hell and Heaven. There are other *distinctions* in life than these. And between all distinctions, between all those differences which separate the "fine" from the "base," the noble from the ignoble, the beautiful from the hideous, the generous from the mean; Dante draws the pitiless sword-stroke of that "eternal separation" which is the most tragic thing in the world. In the truest sense tragic! For so many things, and so many people, that must be thus "cut off," are among those who harrow our hearts with the deadliest attraction and are so wistful in their weakness. Through the mists and mephitic smoke of our confused age—our age that cries out to be beyond the good, when it is beneath the beautiful— through the thick air of indolence masquerading as toleration and indifference posing as sympathy, flashes the scorching sword of the Florentine's Disdain, dividing the just from the unjust, the true from the false, and the heroic from the commonplace. What matter if his "division" is not our "division," his "formula" our "formula"? It is good for us to be confronted with such Disdain. It brings us back once more to "Values"; and whether our "Values" are values of taste or values of devotion what matter? Life becomes once more arresting. The everlasting Drama recovers its "Tone"; and the high Liturgy of the last Illusion rolls forward to its own Music!

That Angel of God, who when their hearts were shaken with fear before the flame-lit walls of Dis, came, so straight across the waters, and quelled the insolence of Hell; with what Disdain he turns away his face, even from those he has come to save!

DANTE

These "messengers" of God, who have so superb a contempt for all created things, does one not meet them, sometimes, even in this life, as they pass us by upon their secret errands?

The beginning of the Inferno contains the cruellest judgment upon our generation ever uttered. It is so exactly adapted to the spirit of this age that, hearing it, one staggers as if from a stab. Are we not this very tribe of caitiffs who have committed the "Great Refusal?" Are we not these very wretches whose blind life is so base that they envy every other Fate? Are we not those who are neither for God or for his Enemies but are "for themselves"; those who may not even take refuge in Hell, lest the one damned get glory of them! The very terror of this clear-cutting sword-sweep, dividing us, bone from bone, may, nay! probably will, send us back to our gentle "lovers of humanity" who, "knowing everything pardon everything." But one sometimes wonders whether a life all "irony," all "pity," all urbane "interest," would not lose the savor of its taste! There is a danger, not only to our moral sense, but to our immoral sense, in that genial air of universal acceptance which has become the fashion.

What if, after all—even though this universe be so poor a farce—the mad lovers and haters, the terrible prophets and artists, *were right?*

VISIONS AND REVISIONS

Suppose the farce had a climax, a catastrophe! One loves to repeat "all is possible;" but *that* particular possibility has little attraction. It would be indeed an anti-climax if the queer Comedy we have so daintily been patronizing turned out to be a Divine Comedy—and ourselves the point of the jest! Not that this is very likely to occur. It is more in accordance with what we know of the terrestial stage that in this wager of faith with un-faith neither will ever discover who really won!

But Dante's "Disdain" is not confined to the winners in the cosmic dicing match. There are heroic hearts in hell who, for all their despair, still yield not, nor abate a jot of their courage. Such a one was that great Ghibelline Chief who was lost for "denying immortality." "If my people fled from thy people—*that* more torments me than this flame." In one respect Dante is, beyond doubt, the greatest poet of the world. I mean in his power of heightening the glory and the terribleness of the human race. Across the three-fold kingdom of his "Terza Rima" passes, in tragic array, the whole procession of human history—and each figure there, each solitary person, whether of the Blessed or the Purged, or the Condemned, wears, like a garment of fire, the dreadful dignity of having been a man! The moving sword-point that flashes, first upon one and then upon another, amid our dim transactions, is nothing but the angry arm of human imagination, moulding life to grander issues; *creating,* if not discovering, sublimer laws.

In conveying that thrilling sense of the momentousness of human destiny which beyond anything else certain historic names evoke, none can surpass him. The brief, branding lines, with which the enemies of God are engraved upon their monuments "more lasting than brass," seem to add a glory to damnation. Who can forget how that "Simonist" and "Son of Sodom" lifts his hands up out of the deepest Pit, and makes "the fig" at God? "Take it, God, for at Thee I aim it!" There is a sting of furious blasphemy in this *personal outrage* that goes beyond all limits.

Yet who is there, but does not feel *glad* that the "Pistoian" uttered what he uttered—out of his Hell—to his Maker?

Is not Newman right when he says that the heart of man does not naturally "love God?"

But perhaps in the whole poem nothing is more beautiful than that great roll of honor of the unchristened Dead, who make up the company of the noble Heathen. Sad, but not unhappy, they walk to and fro in their Pagan Hades, and occupy themselves, as of old, in discoursing upon philosophy and poetry and the Mystery of Life.

Those single lines, devoted to such names, are unlike anything else in literature. That

VISIONS AND REVISIONS

"Caesar, in armour, with Ger-Falcon eyes," challenges one's obeisance as a great shout of his own legionaries, while that "Alone, by himself, the Soldan" bows to the dust our Christian pride, as the Turbaned Commander of the Faithful, with his ghostly crescent blade, strides past, dreaming of the Desert.

It is in touches like these, surely, rather than in the Beatrice scenes or the devil scenes, that the poet is most himself.

It needs, perhaps, a certain smouldering dramatic passion, in regard to the whole spectacle of human life, to do justice to such lines. It needs also that mixture of disdain and humility which is his own paramount attribute.

And the same smouldering furnace of "reverence" characterizes Dante's use of the older literatures. No writer who has ever lived has such a dramatic sense of the "great effects" in style, and the ritual of words.

That passage, *"Thou* art my master and my author. It is from *thee* I learnt the beautiful style that has done me so much honour," with its reiteration of the rhythmic syllables of "honour," opens up a salutary field of æsthetic contemplation. His quotations, too, from the Psalms, and from the Roman Liturgy, become, by their imaginative inclusion, part of his own creative genius. That "Vexilla regis prodeunt Inferni!" Who can hear it without the same thrill, as when Napoleonic

DANTE

trumpets heralded the Emperor! In the presence of such moments the whole elaboration of the Beatrice Cult falls away. That romantic perversion of the sex instinct is but the psychic motive force. Once started on his splendid and terrible road, the poet forgets everything except the "Principle of Beauty" and the "Memory of Great Men." Parallel with these things is Dante's passion of reverence for the old historic places—provinces, cities, rivers and valleys of his native Italy. Even when he lifts up his voice to curse them, as he curses his own Firenze, it is but an inversion of the same mood. The cities where men dwelt then took to themselves living personalities; and Dante, who in love and hate was Italian of the Italians, was left indifferent by none of these. How strange to modern ears this thrill of recognition, when one exile, even among the dead, meets another, of their common citizenship of "no mean city!" Of this classic "patriotism" the world requires a Renaissance, that we may be saved from the shallowness of artificial commercial Empires. The new "Inter-nationalism" is the sinister product of a generation that has grown "deracinated," that has lost its roots in the soil. It is an Anglo-Germanic thing and opposed to it the proud tenacity of the Latin race turns, even today, to what Barrés calls the "worship of one's Dead."

VISIONS AND REVISIONS

Anglo-Saxon Industrialism, Teutonic Organization, have their world place; but it is to the Latin, and, it may be, to the Slav also, that the human spirit must turn in those subtler hours when it cannot "live by bread alone."

The modern international empires may obliterate local boundaries and trample on local altars. In spite of them, and in defiance of them, the soul of an ancient race lives on, its saints and its artists forging the iron of its Phœnix-ashes!

Dante himself, dreaming over the high Virgilian Prophecy of a World-State, under a Spiritual Caesar, yearned to restore the Pax Romana to a chaotic world. Such a vision, such an Orbis Terrarum at the feet of Christ, has no element in common with the material dominance of modern commercial empires. It much more closely resembles certain Utopias of the modern Revolutionary. In its spirit it is not less Latin than the traditional customs of the City-States it would include. Its real implication may be found in the assimilative genius of the Catholic Church, consecrating but not effacing local altars; transforming, but not destroying, local pieties. Who can deny that this formidable vision answers the deepest need of the modern world?

The discovery of some Planetary Synthesis within the circle of which all the passionate race cults may flourish; growing not less intense but more intense, under the new World-City—this is nothing else than what the soul of the earth, "dreaming on things to come," may actually be evolving.

Who knows if the new prominence given by the war to Russian thought may not incredibly hasten such a Vita Nuova? We know that the Pan-Slavic dream, even from the days of Ivan the Terrible, has been of this spiritual unity, and it may be remembered that it was always from "beyond the Alps" that Dante looked for the Liberator. Who knows? The great surging antipodal tides of life lash one another into foam. Out of chaos stars are born. And it may be the madness of a dream even so much as to speak of "unity" while creation seethes and hisses in its terrible vortex. Mockingly laugh the imps of irony, while the Saints keep their vigil. Man is a surprising animal; by no means always bent on his own redemption; sometimes bent on his own destruction!

And meanwhile the demons of life dance on. Dante may build up his great triple universe in his great triple rhyme, and encase it in walls of brass. But still they dance on. We may tremble at the supreme poet's pride and wonder at the passion of his humility—but "the damned grotesques make arabesques, like the wind upon the sand!"

SHAKESPEARE

SHAKESPEARE

THERE is something pathetic about the blind devotion of humanity to its famous names. But how indiscriminate it is; how lacking in discernment!

This is, above all, true of Shakespeare, whose peculiar and quite personal genius has almost been buried under the weight of popular idolatry. No wonder such critics as Voltaire, Tolstoi, and Mr. Bernard Shaw have taken upon themselves to intervene. The Frenchman's protest was an aesthetic one. The more recent objectors have adopted moral and philosophic grounds. But it is the unreasoning adoration of the mob which led to both attacks.

It is not difficult to estimate the elements which have gone to make up this Shakespeare-God. The voices of the priests behind the Idol are only too clearly distinguishable. We hear the academic voice, the showman's voice, and the voice of the ethical preacher. They are all absurd, but their different absurdities have managed to flow together into one powerful and unified convention. Our popular orators gesticulate and clamour; our professors "talk Greek;" our ethical Brutuses "explain;" and the mob "throw up their sweaty night-caps;" while our poor Caesar of Poetry sinks down out of sight, helpless among them all.

Charles Lamb, who understood him better than anyone—and who loved Plays—does not hesitate to accuse our Stage-Actors of being the worst of all in their misrepresentation. He doubts whether even Garrick understood the subtlety of the rôles he played, and the few exceptions he allows in his own age make us wonder what he would say of ours.

Finally there is the "Philosophical Shakespeare" of the German appreciation, and this we feel instinctively to be the least like the original of all!

The irony of it is that the author of Hamlet and the Tempest does not only live in a different world from that of these motley exponents. He lives in an antagonistic one. Shakespeare was as profoundly the enemy of scholastic pedantry as he was the enemy of puritan squeamishness. He was almost unkindly averse to the breath of the profane crowd. And his melancholy scepticism, with its half-humorous assent to the traditional pieties, is at the extremest opposite pole from the "truths" of metaphysical reason. The Shakespeare of the Popular Revivals is a fantastic caricature. The Shakespeare of the Col-

SHAKESPEARE

lege Text-Books is a lean scarecrow. But the Shakespeare of the philosophical moralists is an Hob-goblin from whom one flees in dismay.

Enjoying the plays themselves—the interpreters forgotten—a normally intelligent reader cannot fail to respond to a recognisable Personality there, a Personality with apathies and antipathies, with prejudices and predilections. Very quickly he will discern the absurd unreality of that monstrous Idol, that ubiquitous Hegelian God. Very soon he will recognize that in trying to make their poet everything they have made him nothing.

No one can read Shakespeare with direct and simple enjoyment without discovering in his plays a quite definite and personal attitude towards life. Shakespeare is no Absolute Divinity, reconciling all oppositions and transcending all limitations. He is not that "cloud-capped mountain," too lofty to be scanned, of Matthew Arnold's Sonnet. He is a sad and passionate artist, using his bitter experiences to intensify his insight, and playing with his humours and his dreams to soften the sting of that brutish reality which he was doomed to unmask. The best way of indicating the personal mood which emerges as his final attitude is to describe it as that of the perfectly natural man confronting the universe. Of course, there is no such "perfectly natural man," but he is a legitimate lay-figure, and we all approximate to him at times. The natural man, in his unsophisticated hours, takes the Universe at its surface value, neither rejecting the delicate compensations, nor mitigating the cruelty of the grotesque farce. The natural man accepts *what is given.* He swallows the chaotic surprises, the extravagant accidents, the whole fantastic "pell-mell." He accepts, too, the traditional pieties of his race, their "hope against hope," their gracious ceremonial, their consecration of birth and death. He accepts these, not because he is confident of their "truth," but because *they are there;* because they have been there so long, and have interwoven themselves with the chances and changes of the whole dramatic spectacle.

He accepts them spontaneously, humorously, affectionately; not anxious to improve them —what would be the object of that?—and certainly not seeking to controvert them. He reverences this Religion of his Race not only because it has its own sad, pathetic beauty, but because it has got itself involved in the common burden; lightening such a burden here, making it, perhaps, a little heavier there, but lending it a richer tone, a subtler colour, a more significant shape. It does not trouble the natural man that Religion should deal with "the Impossible." Where, in such a world as this, does *that* begin? He has no agitating desire to reconcile it with reason.

SHAKESPEARE

At the bottom of his soul he has a shrewd suspicion that it rather grew out of the earth than fell from the sky, but that does not concern him. It may be based upon no eternal verity. It may lead to no certain issue. It may be neither very "useful" or very "moral." But it is, at any rate, a beautiful work of imaginative art, and it lends life a certain dignity that nothing can quite replace. As a matter of fact, the natural man's attitude to these things does not differ much from the attitude of the great artists. It is only that a certain lust for creation, and a certain demonic curiosity, scourge these latter on to something beyond passive resignation.

A De Vinci or a Goethe accepts religion and uses it, but between it and the depths of his own mind remains forever an inviolable film of sceptical "white light." This "qualified assent" is precisely what excites the fury of such individualistic thinkers as Tolstoi and Bernard Shaw. It were amusing to note the difference between the "humour" of this latter and the "humour" of Shakespeare. Shaw's humour consists in emphasizing the absurdity of human Custom, compared with the good sense of the philosopher. Shakespeare's humour consists in emphasizing the absurdity of philosophers, compared with the good sense of Custom. The one is the humour of the Puritan, directed against the ordinary man, on behalf of the Universe. The other is the humour of the Artist, directed against the Universe, on behalf of the ordinary man.

Shakespeare is, at bottom, the most extreme of Pessimists. He has no faith in "progress," no belief in "eternal values," no transcendental "intuitions," no zeal for reform. The universe to him, for all its loveliness, remains an outrageous jest. The cosmic is the comic. Anything may be expected of this "pendant world," except what we expect; and when it is a question of "falling back," we can only fall back on human-made custom. We live by Illusions, and when the last Illusion fails us, we die. After reading Shakespeare, the final impression left upon the mind is that the world can only be justified as an aesthetic spectacle. To appreciate a Show at once so sublime and so ridiculous, one needs to be very brave, very tender, and very humorous. Nothing else is needed. "Man must abide his going hence, even as his coming hither. Ripeness is all." When Courage fails us, it is—"as flies to wanton boys are we to the gods. They kill us for their sport." When tenderness fails us, it is—"Tomorrow and tomorrow and tomorrow, creeps in this petty pace from day to day to the last syllable of recorded time." When humour fails us, it is—"How weary, stale, flat and unprofitable, seem to me all the uses of this world!"

SHAKESPEARE

So much for Life! And when we come to Death, how true it is, as Charles Lamb says, that none has spoken of Death like Shakespeare! And he has spoken of it so—with such an absolute grasp of our mortal feeling about it—because his mood in regard to it is the mood of the natural man; of the natural man, unsophisticated by false hopes, unelated by vain assurance. His attitude towards death neither sweetens "the unpalatable draught of mortality" nor permits us to let go the balm of its "eternal peace." How frightful "to lie in cold obstruction and to rot; this sensible warm motion to become a kneaded clod!" and yet, "after life's fitful fever," how blessed to "sleep well!"

What we note about this mood—the mood of Shakespeare and the natural man—is that it never for a moment dallies with philosophic fancies or mystic visions. It "thinks highly of the soul," but in the natural, not the metaphysical, sense. It is the attitude of Rabelais and Montaigne, not the attitude of Wordsworth or Browning. It is the tone we know so well in the Homeric poems. It is the tone of the Psalms of David. We hear its voice in "Ecclesiastes," and the wisdom of "Solomon the King" is full of it. In more recent times, it is the feeling of those who veer between our race's traditional hope and the dark gulf of eternal silence. It is the "Aut Christus aut

Nihil" of those who "by means of metaphysic" have dug a pit, into which metaphysic has disappeared!

The gaiety and childlike animal spirits of Shakespeare's Comedies need not deceive us. Why should we not forget the whips and scorns for a while, and fleet the time carelessly, "as they did in the golden age?" Such simple fooling goes better with the irresponsibility of our fate than the more pungent wit of the moral comedians. The tragic laughter which the confused issues of life excite in subtler souls is not lacking, but the sweet obliquities of honest clowns carry us just as far. Shakespeare loves fools as few have loved them, and it is often his humour to put into their mouth the ultimate wisdom.

It is remarkable that these plays should commence with a "Midsummer Night's Dream" and end with a "Tempest." In the interval the great sombre passions of our race are sounded and dismissed; but as he began with Titania, so he ends with Ariel. From the fairy forest to the enchanted island; from a dream to a dream. With Shakespeare there is no Wagnerian, Euripidean "apologia." There is no "Parsifal" or "Bacchanals." From the meaningless tumult of mortal passions he returns, with a certain ironic weariness, to the magic of Nature and the wonder of youth. Prospero, dismissing his spirits "into thin air," has

SHAKESPEARE

the last word; and the last word is as the first: "we are such stuff as dreams are made on, and our little life is rounded with a sleep." The easy-going persons who reluct at the idea of a pessimistic Shakespeare should turn the pages of Troilus and Cressida, Measure for Measure, and Timon of Athens. What we guessed as we read Hamlet and Lear grows a certainty as we read these plays.

Here the "gentle Shakespeare" does the three things that are most unpardonable. He unmasks virtue; he betrays Woman; and he curses the gods. The most intransigeant of modern revolutionaries might learn a trick or two from this sacred poet. In Lear he puts the very voice of Anarchy into the mouth of the King—"Die for adultery? No!" "Handy-dandy, which is the Magistrate and which is the Thief?" "A dog's obeyed in office."

Have I succeeded in making clear what I feel about the Shakespearean attitude? At bottom, it is absolutely sceptical. Deep yawns below Deep; and if we cannot read "the writing upon the wall," the reason may be that there is no writing there. Having lifted a corner of the Veil of Isis, having glanced once into that Death-Kingdom where grope the roots of the Ash-Tree whose name is Fear, we return to the surface, from Nadir to Zenith, and become "superficial"—"out of profundity."

The infinite spaces, as Pascal said, are

"frightful." That way madness lies. And those who would be sane upon earth must drug themselves with the experience, or with the spectacle of the experience, of human passion. Within this charmed circle, and here alone, they may be permitted to forget the Outer Terror.

The noble spirit is not the spirit that condescends to pamper in itself those inflated moods of false optimistic hope, which, springing from mere physiological well-being, send us leaping and bounding, with such boisterous assurance, along the sunny road. Such pragmatic self-deception is an impertinence in the presence of a world like this.

It is a sign of what one might call a philosophically ill-bred nature. It is the indecent "gratitude" of the pig over his trough. It is the little yellow eye of sanctified bliss turned up to the God who *"must* be in His Heaven" if *we* are so privileged. This "never doubting good will triumph" is really, when one examines it, nothing but the inverted prostration of the helot-slave, glad to have been allowed to get so totally drunk! It blusters and swaggers, but at heart it is base and ignoble. For it is not sensitive enough to feel that the Universe *cannot be pardoned* for the cry of one tortured creature, and that all "the worlds we shall traverse" cannot make up for the despair of one human child.

SHAKESPEARE

To be "cheerful" about the Universe in the manner of these people is to insult the Christ who died. It is to outrage the "little ones," over whose bodies the Wheel has passed. When Nietzsche, the martyr of his own murdered pity, calls upon us to "love Fate," he does not shout so lustily. His laughter is the laughter of one watching his darling stripped for the rods. He who would be "in harmony with Nature," with those "murderous ministers," who, in their blind abyss, throw dice with Chance, must be in harmony with the giants of Jotunheim, as well as with the lords of Valhalla. He must be able to look on grimly while Asgard totters; he must welcome "the Twilight of the Gods." To have a mind inured to such conceptions, a mind capable of remaining on such a verge, is, alone, to be, intellectually speaking, what we call "aristocratic." When, even with eyes like poor Gloucester's in the play, we can see "how this world wags," it is slavish and "plebeian" to swear that it all "means intensely, and means well." It is also to lie in one's throat!

No wonder Shakespeare treats reverently every "superstition," every anodyne and nepenthe offered to the inmates of this House of the Incurable. Such "sprinkling with holy water," such "rendering ourselves stupid," is the only alternative. Anything else is the insight of the hero, or the hypocrisy of the preacher!

Has it been realized how curiously the interpreters of Shakespeare omit the principal thing?

They revel in his Grammar, his History, his Biology, his Botany, his Geography, his Psychology and his Ethics. They never speak of his Poetry. Now Shakespeare is, above everything, a poet. To poetry, over and over again, as our Puritans know well, he sacrifices Truth, Morality, Probability, nay! the very principles of Art itself.

As Dramas, many of his plays are scandalously bad; many of his characters fantastic. One can put one's finger in almost every case upon the persons and situations that interested him and upon those that did not. And how carelessly he "sketches in" the latter! So far from being "the Objective God of Art" they seek to make him, he is the most wayward and subjective of all wandering souls.

No natural person can read him without feeling the pulse of extreme personal passion behind everything he writes.

And this pulse of personal passion is always expressing itself in Poetry. He will let the probabilities of a character vanish into air, or dwindle into a wistful note of attenuated convention, when once such a one has served his purpose as a reed to pipe his strange tunes

SHAKESPEARE

through. He will whistle the most important personage down the wind, lost to interest and identity, when once he has put into his mouth his own melancholy brooding upon life—his own imaginative reaction.

And so it happens that, in spite of all academic opinion, those who understand Shakespeare best tease themselves least over his dramatic lapses. For let it be whispered at once, without further scruple. As far as *the art of the drama* is concerned, Shakespeare is *shameless*. The poetic instinct—one might call it "epical" or "lyrical," for it is both these—is far more dominant in our "greatest dramatist" than any dramatic conscience. That is precisely why those among us who love "poetry," but find "drama," especially "drama since Ibsen," intolerably tiresome, revert again and again to Shakespeare. Only absurd groups of Culture-Philistines can read these "powerful modern productions" more than once! One knows not whether their impertinent preaching, or their exasperating technical cleverness is the more annoying.

They may well congratulate themselves on being different from Shakespeare. They are extremely different. They are, indeed, nothing but his old enemies, the Puritans, "translated," like poor Bottom, and wearing the donkey's head of "art for art's sake" in place of their own simple foreheads.

Art for art's sake! The thing has become a Decalogue of forbidding commandments, as devastating as *those Ten*. It is the new avatar of the "moral sense" carrying categorical insolence into the sphere of our one Alsatian sanctuary!

I am afraid Shakespeare was a very "immoral" artist. I am afraid he wrote as one of the profane.

But what of the Greeks? The Greeks never let themselves go! No! And for a sufficient reason. Greek Drama was Religion. It was Ritual. And we know how "responsible" ritual must be. The gods must have their incense from the right kind of censer.

But you cannot evoke Religion "in vacuo." You cannot, simply by assuming grave airs about your personal "taste," or even about the "taste" of your age, give it *that consecration*.

Beauty? God knows what beauty is. But I can tell you what it is not. It is not the sectarian anxiety of any pompous little clique to get "saved" in the artistic "narrow path." It is much rather what Stendhal called it. But he spoke so frivolously that I dare not quote him.

Has it occurred to you, gentle reader, to note how "Protestant" this New Artistic Movement is? Shakespeare, in his aesthetic method, as well as in his piety, had a Catholic soul. In truth, the hour has arrived when a "Renaissance" of the free spirit of Poetry in Drama is required. Why must this monstrous shadow of the Hyperborean Ibsen go on darkening the play-instinct in us, like some ugly, domineering John Knox? I suspect that there are many generous Rabelaisian souls who could lift our mortal burden with oceanic merriment, only the New Movement frightens them. They are afraid they would not be "Greek" enough—or "Scandinavian" enough. Meanwhile the miserable populace have to choose between Babylonian Pantomimes and Gaelic Mythology, if they are not driven, out of a kind of spite, into the region of wholesome "domestic sunshine."

What, in our hearts, we natural men desire is to be delivered at one blow from the fairies with weird names (so different from poor Titania!), and from the three-thousand "Unities!" What "poetry" we do get is so vague and dim and wistful and forlorn that it makes us want to go out and "buy clothes" for someone. We veer between the abomination of city-reform and the desolation of Ultima Thule.

But Shakespeare is Shakespeare still. O those broken and gasped-out human cries, full of the old poignancy, full of the old enchantment! Shakespeare's poetry is the extreme opposite of any "cult." It is the ineffable expression, in music that makes the heart stop, of the feelings which have stirred every Jack and Jill among us, from the beginning of the world! It has the effect of those old "songs" of the countryside that hit the heart in us so shrewdly that one feels as though the wind had made them or the rain or the wayside grass; for they know too much of what we tell to none! It is the "one touch of Nature." And how they break the rules, these surpassing lines, in which the emotions of his motley company gasp themselves away!

It is not so much in the great speeches, noble as these are, as in the brief, tragic cries and broken stammerings, that his unapproachable felicity is found. "Upon such sacrifices, my Cordelia, the gods themselves throw incense." Thick and fast they crowd upon our memory, these little sentences, these aching rhythms! It is with the flesh and blood of the daily Sacrifice of our common endurance that he celebrates his strange Mass. Hands that "smell of mortality," lips that "so sweetly were forsworn," eyes that "look their last" on all they love, these are the touches that make us bow down before the final terrible absolution. And it is the same with Nature. Not to Shakespeare do we go for those pseudo-scientific, pseudo-ethical interpretations, so crafty in their word-painting, so cunning in their rational analysis, which we find in the rest. A few fierce-flung words, from the hot heart of

SHAKESPEARE

an amorist's lust, and all the smouldering magic of the noon-day woods takes your breath. A sobbing death-dirge from the bosom of a love-lorn child, and the perfume of all the "enclosed gardens" in the world shudders through your veins.

And what about the ancient antagonist of the Earth? What about the Great Deep? Has anyone, anywhere else, gathered into words the human tremor and the human recoil that are excited universally when we go down "upon the beached verge of the salt flood, who once a day with his embossed froth the turbulent surge doth cover?" John Keats was haunted day and night by the simple refrain in Lear, "Canst thou not hear the Sea?"

Charming Idyllists may count the petals of the cuckoo-buds in the river-pastures; and untouched, we admire. But let old Falstaff, as he lies a'dying, "babble o' green fields," and all the long, long thoughts of youth steal over us, like a summer wind.

The modern critic, with a philosophic bias, is inclined to quarrel with the obvious human congruity of Shakespeare's utterances. What is the *use* of this constant repetition of the obvious truism: "When we are born we cry that we are come to this great stage of fools?"

No use, my friend! No earthly use! And yet it is not a premeditated reflection, put in "for art's sake." It is the poetry of the pinch of Fate; it is the human revenge we take upon the insulting irony of our lot.

But Shakespeare does not always strike back at the gods with bitter blows. In this queer world, where we have "nor youth, nor age, but, as it were, an after-dinner's sleep, dreaming on both," there come moments when the spirit is too sore wounded even to rise in revolt. Then, in a sort of "cheerful despair," we can only wait the event. And Shakespeare has his word for this also.

Perhaps the worst of all "the slings and arrows" are the intolerable partings we have to submit to, from the darlings of our soul. And here, while he offers us no false hope, his tone loses its bitterness, and grows gentle and solemn.

It is—"Forever and forever, farewell, Cassius. If we do meet again, why then 'tis well; if not, this parting was well made." And for the Future:

"O that we knew
The end of this day's business ere it comes!
But it suffices that the day will end;
And then the end is known."

EL GRECO

EL GRECO

HE emerging of a great genius into long retarded pre-eminence is always attended by certain critical misunderstandings. To a cynical observer, on the lookout for characteristic temperamental lapses, two recent interpretations of El Greco may be especially commended. I mean the *Secret of Toledo,* by Maurice Barrés, and an article in the "Contemporary" of April, 1914, by Mr. Aubrey Bell.

Barrés—Frenchman of Frenchmen—sets off, with captivating and plausible logic, to generalize into reasonable harmlessness this formidable madman. He interprets Toledo, appreciates Spain, and patronizes Domenico Theotocopoulos.

The *Secret of Toledo* is a charming book, with illuminating passages, but it is too logical, too plausible, too full of the preciosity of dainty generalization, to reach the dark and arbitrary soul, either of Spain or of Spain's great painter.

Mr. Bell, on the contrary, far from turning

El Greco into an epicurean cult, drags him with a somewhat heavy hand before the footlights of English Idealism.

He makes of him an excuse for disparaging Velasquez, and launches into a discourse upon the Higher Reality and the Inner Truth which leaves one with a very dreary feeling, and, by some ponderous application of spiritual ropes and pulleys, seems to jerk into empty space all that is most personal and arresting in the artist.

If it is insulting to the ghostly Toledoan to smooth him out into picturesque harmony with Castillian dances, Gothic cloisters and Moorish songs, it is still worse to transform him into a rampant Idealist of the conventional kind. He belongs neither to the Aesthetics nor to the Idealists. He belongs to every individual soul whose taste is sufficiently purged, sufficiently perverse and sufficiently passionate, to enter the enchanted circle of his tyrannical spell.

When, in that dark Toledo Church, one presses one's face against the iron bars that separate one from the Burial of Count Orguz, it is neither as a Dilettante nor an Idealist that one holds one's breath. Those youthful pontifical saints, so richly arrayed, offering with slender royal hands that beautiful body to the dust—is their mysterious gesture only the rythm of the secret of Death?

Those chastened and winnowed spectators,

with their withdrawn, remote detachment—not sadness—are they the initiated sentinels of the House of Corruption?

At what figured symbol points that epicene child?

Sumptuous is the raiment of the dead; and the droop of his limbs has a regal finality; but look up! Stark naked, and in abandoned weakness, the liberated soul shudders itself into the presence of God!

The El Greco House and Museum in Toledo contains amazing things. Every one of those Apostles that gaze out from the wall upon our casual devotion has his own furtive madness, his own impossible dream! The St. John is a thing one can never forget. El Greco has painted his hair as if it were literally live flame and the exotic tints of his flesh have an emphasis laid upon them that makes one think of the texture of certain wood orchids.

How irrelevant seem Monsieur Barrés' water-colour sketches of prancing Moors and learned Jews and picturesque Visi-Goths, as soon as one gets a direct glimpse into these unique perversions! And why cannot one go a step with this dreamer of dreams without dragging in the Higher Reality? To regard work as mad and beautiful as this as anything but individual Imagination, is to insult the mystery of personality.

VISIONS AND REVISIONS

El Greco re-creates the world, in pure, lonely, fantastic arbitrariness.

His art does not represent the secret Truth of the Universe, or the Everlasting Movement; it represents the humour of El Greco.

Every artist mesmerizes us into his personal vision.

A traveller, drinking wine in one of those cafés in the crowded Zocodover, his head full of these amazing fantasies, might well let the greater fantasy of the world slip by—a dream within a dream!

With El Greco for a companion, the gaunt waiter at the table takes the form of some incarcerated Don Quixote and the beggars at the window appear like gods in disguise.

This great painter, like the Russian Dostoivsky, has a mania for abandoned weakness. The nearer to God his heroic Degenerates get, the more feverishly enfeebled becomes their human will.

Their very faces—with those retreating chins, retroussé noses, loose lips, quivering nostrils and sloping brows—seem to express the abandonment of all human resolution or restraint, in the presence of the Beatific Vision. Like the creatures of Dostoievsky, they seem to plunge into the ocean of the Foolishness of God, so much wiser than the wisdom of men! —as divers plunge into a bath.

There is not much attempt among these ecstatics to hold on to the dignity of their reason or the reticence of their self-respect. Naked, they fling themselves into the arms of Nothingness.

This passionate "Movement of Life," of which Mr. Bell, quoting Pater's famous quotation from Heraclitus, makes so much, is, after all, only the rush of the wind through the garments of the World—Denier, as he plunges into Eternity.

Like St. John of the Cross, El Greco's visionaries pass from the Night of the Reason to the Night of the Senses; from the Night of the Senses to the Night of Soul; and if this final Night is nothing less than God Himself, the divine submersion does not bring back any mortal daylight.

Domenico's portraits have a character somewhat different from his visions. Here, into these elongated, bearded hermits, into these grave, intellectual maniacs, whose look is like the look of Workers in some unlit Mine, he puts what he knows and feels of his own identity.

They are diverse masks and mirrors, these portraits, surfaces of deep water in various lonely valleys, but from the depths of them rises up the shadow of the same lost soul, and they are all ruffled by the breath of the same midnight.

The Crucifixion in the Prado, and that other,

which, by some freak of Providence, has found its way to Philadelphia, have backgrounds which carry our imagination very far. Is this primordial ice, with its livid steel-blue shadows, the stuff out of which the gods make other planets than ours—dead planets, without either sun or star? Are these the sheer precipices of Chaos, against which the Redeemer hangs, or the frozen edges of the grave of all life?

El Greco's magnificent contempt for material truth is a lesson to all artists. We are reminded of William Blake and Aubrey Beardsley. He seems to regard the human frame as so much soft clay, upon which he can trace his ecstatic hieroglyphs, in defiance both of anatomy and nature.

El Greco is the true precursor of our present-day Matissists and Futurists. He, as they, has the courage to strip his imagination of all mechanical restrictions and let it go free to mould the world at its fancy.

What stray visitor to Madrid would guess the vastness of the intellectual sensation awaiting him in that quiet, rose-coloured building?

As you enter the Museum and pass those magnificent Titians crowded so close together —large and mellow spaces, from a more opulent world than ours; greener branches, bluer skies and a more luminous air; a world through which, naturally and at ease, the divine Christ may move, grand, majestic, health-giving, a veritable god; a world from whose grapes the blood of satyrs may be quickened, from whose corn the hearts of heroes may be made strong—and come bolt upon El Greco's glacial northern lights, you feel that no fixed objective Truth and no traditional Ideal has a right to put boundaries to the imagination of man.

Not less striking than any of these is the extraordinary portrait of "Le Roi Ferdinand" in the great gallery at the Louvre.

The artist has painted the king as one grown weary of his difference from other men. His moon-white armour and silvery crown show like the ornaments of the dead. Misty and wavering, the long shadows upon the high, strange brow seem thrown there by the passing of all mortal Illusions.

Phantom-like in his gleaming ornaments, a king of Lost Atlantis, he waits the hour of his release.

And not only is he the king of Shadows; he is also the king of Players, the Player-King.

El Greco has painted him holding two sceptres, one of which, resembling a Fool's Bauble, is tipped with the image of a naked hand—a dead, false hand—symbol of the illusion of Power. The very crown he wears, shimmering and unnaturally heavy, is like the crown a child might have made in play, out of shells and sea-weed.

The disenchanted irony upon the face of this figure; that look as of one who—as Plato would have us do with kings—has been dragged back from Contemplation to the vulgarity of ruling men; has been deliberately blent by a most delicate art with a queer sort of fantastic whimsicality.

"Le Roi Ferdinand" might almost be an enlarged reproduction of some little girl's Doll-King, dressed up in silver tinsel and left out of doors, by mistake, some rainy evening.

Something about him, one fancies, would make an English child think of the "White Knight" in *Alice Through the Looking Glass,* so helpless and simple he looks, this poor "Revenant," propped up by Youthful Imagination, and with the dews of night upon his armour.

You may leave these pictures far behind you as you re-cross the Channel, but you can never quite forget El Greco.

In the dreams of night the people of his queer realm will return and surround you, ebbing and flowing, these passionate shadows, stretching out vain arms after the infinite and crying aloud for the rest they cannot win.

Yes, in the land of dreams we know him, this proud despiser of earth!

From our safe inland retreat we watch the passing of his Dance of Death, and we know

EL GRECO

that what they seek, these wanderers upon the wind, is not our Ideal nor our Real, not our Earth or our Heaven, but a strange, fairy-like Nirvana, where, around the pools of Nothingness, the children of twilight gambol and play.

The suggestive power of genius plays us, indeed, strange tricks. I have sometimes fancied that the famished craving in the eyes and nostrils of El Greco's saints was a queer survival of that tragic look which that earlier Greek, Scopas the Sculptor, took such pains to throw upon the eyelids of his half-human amphibiums.

It might even seem to us, dreaming over these pictures as the gusts of an English autumn blow the fir branches against the window, as though all that weird population of Domenico's brain were tossing their wild, white arms out there and emitting thin, bat-like cries under the drifting moon.

The moon—one must admit that, at least—rather than the sun, was ever the mistress of El Greco's genius. He will come more and more to represent for us those vague uneasy feelings that certain inanimate and elemental objects have the power of rousing. It is of him that one must think, when this or that rock-chasm cries aloud for its Demon, or this or that deserted roadway mutters of its unreturning dead.

There will always be certain great artists,

and they are the most original of all who refuse to submit to any of our logical categories, whether scientific or ideal.

To give one's self up to them is to be led by the hand into the country of Pure Imagination, into the Ultima Thule of impossible dreams.

Like Edgar Allan Poe, this great painter can make splendid use of the human probabilities of Religion and Science; but it is none of these things that one finally thinks, as one comes to follow him, but of things more subtle, more remote, more translunar, and far more imaginative.

One may walk the streets of Toledo to seek the impress of El Greco's going and coming; but the soul of Domenico Theotocopoulos is not there.

It is with Faust, in the cave of the abyssmal "Mothers."

MILTON

MILTON

IT is outrageous, the way we modern world-children play with words. How we are betrayed by words! How we betray with words! We steal from one another and from the spirit of the hour; and with our phrases and formulas and talismans we obliterate all distinction. One sees the modern god as one who perpetually apologises and explains; and the modern devil as one who perpetually apologises and explains. Everything has its word-symbol, its word-mask, its word-garment, its word-disgrace. Nothing comes out clear into the open, unspeakable and inexplicable, and strikes us dumb!

That is what the great artists do—who laugh at our word-play. That is what Milton does, who, in the science and art of handling words, has never been equalled. Milton, indeed, remains, by a curious fate, the only one of the very great poets who has never been "interpreted" or "appreciated" or "re-created" by any critical modern. And they have left him alone; have been frightened of him; have not dared to slime their "words" over him, for the very reason that he is the supreme artist in words! He is so great an artist that his creations detach themselves from all dimness —from all such dimness as modern "appreciation" loves—and stand out clear and cold and "unsympathetic"; to be bowed down before and worshipped, or left unapproached.

Milton is a man's poet. It would be a strange thing if women loved him. Modern criticism is a half-tipsy Hermaphrodite, in love only with what is on the point of turning into something else. Milton is always himself. His works of art are always themselves. He and they are made of the same marble, of the same metal. They are never likely to change into anything else! Milton is, like all the greatest artists, a man of action. He, so learned in words, in their history, in their weight, in their origin, in their evocations; he, the scholar of scholars, is a man, not of words, but of deeds. That is why the style of Milton is a thing that you can touch with your outstretched fingers. It has been hammered into shape by a hand that could grasp a sword; it has been moulded into form by a brain that could dominate a council-chamber. No wonder we word-maniacs fear to approach him. He repels us; he holds us back; he hides his work-shop from us; and his art smites us into silent hatred.

MILTON

For Milton himself, though he is the artist of artists, art is not the first thing. It is only the first thing with us because we are life's slaves, and not its masters. Art is what we protect ourselves with—from life. For us it is a religion and a drug. To Milton it was a weapon and a plaything.

Milton was more interested in the struggle of ideas, in the struggle of races, in the struggle of immortal principles, in the struggle of gods, in the great creative struggle of life and death, than he was interested in the exquisite cadences of words or their laborious arrangement. A modern artist's heart's desire is to escape from the world to some "happy valley" and there, sitting cross-legged, like a Chinese Idol, between the myrtle-bushes and the Lotus, to make beautiful things in detachment forever, one by one, with no pause or pain. Milton's desire was to take the whole round world between his hands, with all the races and nations who dwell upon it, and mould *that,* and nothing less, into the likeness of what he believed. And in what did he believe, this Lord of Time and Space, this accomplice of Jehovah? He believed in Himself. He had the unquestioning, unphilosophical belief in himself which great men of action have; which the Caesars, Alexanders and Napoleons have, and which Shakespeare seems to have lacked.

Milton, though people have been misled into

thinking of him as very different from that, was, in reality, the incarnation of the Nietzschean ideal. He was hard, he was cold, he was contemptuous, he was "magnanimous," he "remembered his whip" when he went with women, he loved "war" for its own sake, and he dwelt alone on the top of the mountains. To Milton the world presented itself as a place where the dominant power, and the dominant interest, was the wrestling of will with will. Why need we always fuss ourselves about logical *names?* Milton, in reality—in his temperament and his mood—was just as convinced of *Will* being the ultimate secret as Schopenhauer or Nietzsche or Bergson or the modern Pragmatist. Nothing seemed to him noble, or dramatic, or "true," that did not imply the struggle to the death of opposing *wills.*

Milton, in reality, is less of a Christian than any European writer, since the Gospel appeared. In his heart, like Nietzsche, he regarded the binding into one volume of those "Two Testaments" an insult to "the great style." He does, indeed, in a manner find a place for Christ, but it is the place of one demigod among many other demi-gods; the conqueror's place possibly, but still the place of one in a hierarchy, not of one alone. It is absurd to quarrel with Milton's deification of the Judaic Jehovah. Every man has his own God. The God he *has a right to.* And the

MILTON

Jewish Jehovah, after all, is no mean Figure. He, like Milton, was a God of War. He, like Milton, found "Will"—human and divine "Will"—the central cosmic fact. He, like Milton, regarded Good and Evil, not as universal principles, but as arbitrary *commands,* issued by eternal personal antagonists! It is one of the absurd mistakes into which our "conceptual" and "categorical" minds so easily fall—this tendency to eliminate Milton's Theology as mere Puritanical convention, dull and uninteresting. Milton's Theology was the most *personal creation* that any great poet has ever dared to launch upon—more personal even than the Theology of Milton's favourite Greek poet, Euripides.

Milton's feeling for the more personal, more concrete aspects of "God" goes entirely well with the rest of his philosophy. He was, at heart, a savage Dualist, who lapsed occasionally into Pluralism. He was, above all, an Individualist of the most extreme kind—an Individualist so hard, so positive, so inflexible, that for him nothing in the world really mattered or counted except the clash of definite, clear-cut "Wills," contending against one another.

Milton is the least mystical, the least Pantheistic, the least Monistic, of all writers. That magical sense of the brooding Over-Soul which thrills us so in Goethe's poetry never touches his pages. The Wordsworthian intimations of "something far more deeply interfused" never crossed his sensibility; and, as far as he is concerned, Plato might never have existed.

One feels, as one reads Milton, that his ultimate view of the universe is a great chaotic battlefield, amid the confused elements of which rise up the portentous figures of "Thrones, Dominations, Principalities, and Powers," and in the struggle between these, the most arbitrary, the most tyrannical, the most despotic, conquers the rest, and, planting his creative Gonfalon further in the Abyss than any, becomes "God"; the God whose personal and unrestrained Caprice creates the Sun, the Moon and the Stars, out of Chaos; and Man out of the dust of the Earth. Thus it is brought about that what this God *wills* is "Good," and what his strongest and most formidable antagonist wills is "Evil." Between Good and Evil there is no eternal difference, except in the eternal difference between the conquering Personality of Jehovah and the conquered Personality of Lucifer. So, far from it being true that Milton is the dull transcriber of mere traditional Protestantism, a very little investigation reveals the astounding fact that the current popular Evangelical view of the origin of things and the drama of things is based, not upon the Bible at all, but upon Milton's poem. In this respect he is a true Classic Poet—a Maker of Mythology—a Delphic Demiurge.

One of the most difficult questions in the world to answer would be the question how far Milton "believed," simply and directly, in the God he thus half-created. Probably he did "believe" more than his daring, arbitrary "creations" would lead us to suppose. His nature demanded positive and concrete facts. Scepticism and mysticism were both abhorrent to him; and it is more likely than not that, in the depths of his strange cold, unapproachable heart, a terrible and passionate prayer went up, day and night, to the God of Isaac and Jacob that the Lord should not forget his Servant.

The grandeur and granite-like weight of Milton's learning was fed by the high traditions of Greece and Rome; but, in his heart of hearts, far deeper than anything that moved him in Aeschylus or Virgil, was the devotion he had for the religion of Israel, and the Fear of Him who "sitteth between the Cherubims." It is often forgotten, amid the welter of modern ethical ideals and modern mystical theosophies, how grand and unique a thing is this Religion of Israel—a religion whose God is at once Personal and Invisible. After all, what do we know? A Prince of Righteousness, a King of Sion, a Shepherd of his People—such a "Living God" as David cries out upon, with those dramatic cries that remain until today the most human and tragic of all our race's wrestling with the Unknown—is this not a Faith quite as "possible" and far more moving, than all the "Over-Souls" and "Immanent All-Fathers" and "Streams of Tendency" which have been substituted for it by unimaginative modern "breadth of mind"? It is time that it was made clear that the alternative at present for all noble souls is between the reign of "crass Casuality" and the reign of Him "who maketh the clouds His chariot and walketh upon the wings of the wind." Those who, "with Democritus, set the world upon Chance" have a right to worship their Jesus of Nazareth, and, in him, the Eternal Protest against the Cruelty of Life. But if Life is to be deified, if Life is to be "accepted," if Life is to be worshipped; if Courage, not Love, be the secret of the cosmic system, then let us call aloud upon it, under personal and palpable symbols, in the old imaginative, *poetic* way, rather than fool ourselves with thin mysticities, vague intuitions, and the "sounding brass" "ethical ideals"!

The earlier poems of Milton are among the most lovely in the English language. Lycidas is, for those who understand what poetry means, the most lovely of all. There is nothing, anywhere, quite like this poem. The lingering, elaborate harmonies, interrupted in pause after pause, by lines of reverberating finality; and yet, sweetly, slowly leading on to a climax of such airy, lucid calm—it is one's "hope beyond hope" of what a poem should be.

The absence of vulgar sentiment, the classic reserve, the gentle melancholy, the delicate gaiety, the subtle interweaving of divine, rhythmic cadences, the ineffable lightness of touch, as of cunning fingers upon reluctant clay; is there anything in poetry to equal these things? One does not even regret the sudden devastating apparition of that "two-handed engine at the door." For one remembers how wickedly, how mercilessly, the beauty of life is even now being spoiled by these accursed "hirelings"—and now, as then, "nothing said."

The Nativity Hymn owes half the charm of its easy, natural grace to the fact that the victory of Mary's infant son over the rest is treated as if it were the victory of one pagan god over another—the final triumph being to him who is the most "gentle" and "beautiful" of all the gods. In the famous argument between the Lady and her Tempter, in Comus, we have an exquisite example of the sweet, grave refinement of virginal taste which shuns grossness as "a false note." The doctrine of Comus—if so airy a thing can be supposed to have a doctrine—is not very different from the doctrine of Marius the Epicurean. One were foolish to follow the bestial enchanter; not so much because it is "wrong" to do so, as because, then, one would lose the finer edge of that heavenly music which turns the outward shape "to the soul's essence."

Milton's Sonnets occupy a place by themselves in English Literature, and they may well be pondered upon by those who think that the relinquishing of the "old forms" makes it easier to express one's personality. It makes it, as a matter of fact, much harder, just as the stripping from human beings of their characteristic "outer garments" makes them so dreadfully, so devastatingly, alike! Nothing could be more personal than a Miltonic Sonnet. The rigid principles of form, adhered to so scrupulously in the medium used, intensify, rather than detract from, his individualistic character. That Miltonic wit, so granite-like and mordant, how well it goes with the magical whispers that "syllable men's names"!

All Milton's personal prejudices may be found in the Sonnets, from his hatred of those frightful Scotch appelations that would "make Quintlian gasp" to his longing for Classic companionship and "Attic wine" and "immortal notes" and "Tuscan airs"! As one reads on, laughing gently at the folly of those who have so misunderstood him, one is conscious more and more of that high, cold, clear, lonely tenderness, which found so little satisfaction

MILTON

in the sentiment of the rabble and still less in the endearments of women! As in the case of "sad Electra's poet," his own favorite, it is easy to grow angry about his "Misogyny," and take Christian exception to his preference for mistresses over wives. It is true that Milton's view of marriage is more than "heathen." But one has to remember that in these matters of purely personal taste no public opinion has right to intervene. When the well-married Brownings of our age succeed in writing poetry in the "grand style," it will be time—and, perhaps, not even then—to let the dogs of democratic domesticity loose upon this austere lover of the classic way.

What a retort was "Paradise Lost" to the lewd revellers who would have profaned his aristocratic isolation with howlings and brutalities and philistine uproar! Milton despised "priests and kings" from the heights of a pride loftier than their own—and he did not love the vulgar mob much better. In Paradise Lost he can "feel himself" into the sublime tyranny of God, as well as into the sublime revolt of Lucifer. Neither the one or other stoops to solicit "popular voices." The thing to avoid, as one reads this great poem, are the paraphrases from the book of Genesis. Here some odd scrupulousness of scholarly conscience seems to prevent him launching out into his native originality. But, putting this aside, what majestic Pandemoniums of terrific Imagination he has the power to call up! The opening Books are as sublime as the book of Job, and more arresting than Aeschylus. The basic secrets of his blank verse can never be revealed, but one is struck dumb with wonder in the presence of this Eagle of Poetry as we attempt to follow him, flight beyond flight, hovering beyond hovering, as he gets nearer and nearer to the Sun.

It is by single paragraphs, all the same, and by single lines, that I would myself prefer to see him judged. Long poems have been written before and will be written again, but no one will ever write—no one but Dante has ever written—such single lines as one reads in Milton. Curiously enough, some of the most staggering of these superb passages are interludes and allusions, rather than integral episodes in the story, and not only interludes, but interludes in the "pagan manner." Second only to those Luciferan defiances, which seem able to inspire even us poor worms with the right attitude towards Fate, I am tempted to place certain references to Astarte, Ashtoreth and Adonis.

"Astarte, queen of Heaven, with crescent
    horns, ,
To whose bright Image nightly, by the moon,
Sidonian virgins paid their vows and songs."

MILTON

Or of Adonis:
"Whose annual wound, in Lebanon, allured
The Syrian damsels to lament his fate
In amorous ditties all a Summer's day—"
That single line, "Whose annual wound, in Lebanon, allured," seems to me better than any other that could be quoted, to evoke the awe and the thrill and the seduction of all true poetry.

Then those great mysterious allusions to the planetary orbits and the fixed stars and the primeval spaces of land and sea; what a power they have of spreading wide before us the huge horizons of the world's edge! Who can forget "the fleecy star that bears Andromeda far off Atlantic seas"? Or that phrase about the sailors "stemming mightly to the pole"? Or the sudden terror of that guarded Paradisic Gate—"with dreadful faces thronged and fiery arms"? The same extraordinary beauty of single passages may be found in "Paradise Regained," a poem which is much finer than many guess. The descriptions there of the world-cities, Athens, Rome, Jerusalem, have the same classic thrill of reserved awe and infinite reverence that some of Dante's lines possess—only, with Milton, the thing is longer drawn out and more grandiloquent. Satan's speech about his own implacable fatality, "his harbour, and his ultimate repose," and that allusion to Our Lord's gentleness, like "the cool intermission of a summer's cloud," are both in the manner we love.

It is only, however, when one comes to Samson Agonistes that the full power of Milton's genius is felt. Written in a style which the devotees of "free verse" in our time would do well to analyse, it is the most complete expression of his own individual character that he ever attained. Here the Captain of Jehovah, here the champion of Light against Darkness, of Pride against Humility, of Man against Woman, finds his opportunity and his hour. Out of his blindness, out of his loneliness, out of the welter of hedonists and amorists and feminists and fantasists who crowded upon him, the great, terrible egoist strikes his last blow! No one can read Samson Agonistes without being moved, and those who look deepest into our present age may well be moved the most! One almost feels as if some great overpowering tide of all the brutalities and crudities and false sentiments and cunning hypocrisies, and evil voluptuousness, of all the Philistias that have ever been, is actually rushing to overwhelm us! Gath and Askalon in gross triumph—must this thing be? Will the Lord of Hosts lift no finger to help his own? And then the end comes; and the Euripidean "messenger" brings the great news! He is dead, our Champion; but in his death he slew more than in his life. "Nothing is here" for unworthy sorrow; "nothing" that need make us "knock the breast;"—"No weakness, no contempt, dispraise or blame—nothing but well and fair, and what may quiet us in a death so noble."

And the end of Samson Agonistes is as the end of Milton's own life. Awaited in calm dignity, as a Roman soldier might wait for Caesar's word, Death has claimed its own. But let not the "daughters of the uncircumsized" triumph! Grandeur and nobility, beauty and heroism, live still; and while these live, what matter though our bravest and our fairest perish? It only remains to let the thunderbolt, when it does fall, find us prepared; find us in calm of mind, "all passion spent."

CHARLES LAMB

CHARLES LAMB

CHARLES LAMB occupies a very curious position in English literature and a very enviable one. He is, perhaps, the most widely known, and widely spoken of, of any stylist we possess, and the least understood. It was his humour, while living, to create misunderstanding, and he creates it still. And yet he is recognized on all sides as a Classic of the unapproachable breed. Charles Lamb has among his admirers more uninteresting people than any great artist has ever had except Thackeray. He has more academic people in his train than anyone has ever had except Shakespeare. And more severe, elderly, pedantic persons profess to love him than love any other mortal writer.

These people all read Lamb, talk Lamb, quote Lamb, but they do not *suggest* Lamb; they do not "smack," as our ancestors used to say, of the true Elia vein.

But the immense humour of the situation does not stop here. Not only has this evasive City Clerk succeeded in fooling the "good people;" he has fooled the "wicked ones." I have myself in the circle of my acquaintance more than half a dozen charming people, of the type who enjoy Aubrey Beardsley, and have a mania for Oscar Wilde, and sometimes dip into Remy de Gourmont, and not one of them "can read" Charles Lamb. He has succeeded in fooling them; in making them suppose he is something quite different from what he is. He used to tell his friends that every day he felt himself growing more "official" and "moral." He even swore he had been taken for a Verger or a Church warden. Well, our friends of the "enclosed gardens" still take him for a Verger. But he is a more remarkable Verger than they dream. As a matter of fact, there were some extremely daring and modern spirits in Elia's "entourage," spirits who went further in an antinomian direction than—I devoutly pray—my friends are ever likely to go, and these scandalous ones adored him. And for his part, he seems to have liked them—more than he ought.

It is, indeed, very curious and interesting, the literary fate of Charles Lamb. Jocular Bishops, archly toying Rural Deans, Rectors with a "penchant" for anecdote, scholarly Canons with a weakness for Rum Punch, are all inclined to speak as if in some odd way he was of their own very tribe. He had absolutely nothing in common with them, except a talent for giving false impressions! With re-

CHARLES LAMB

gard to the devotion to him which certain gentle and old-fashioned ladies have—one's great-aunts, for instance—I am inclined to think that much more might be said. There is a quality, a super-refined, exquisite quality, and one with a pinch of true ironic salt in it, which the more thick-skinned among us sensationalists may easily miss.

It is all very well for us to talk of "burning with a hard gem-like flame," when, as a matter of fact, we move along, dull as cave-men, to some of the finest aesthetic effects in the world. Not to appreciate the humour of that rarest and sweetest of all human types, the mischievous-tongued Great-Aunt, is to be nothing short of a profane fool.

But Charles Lamb is a very different person from our Goldsmiths and Cowpers and Austens, and their modern representatives. It needs something else in a Great-Aunt than old-fashioned irony to appreciate *him*. It needs an imagination that is very nearly "Shakespearean," and it needs a passion for beautiful style of which a Flaubert or an Anatole France might be proud.

So here we have the old sly Elia, fooling people now as he fooled them in his lifetime, and a riddle both to the godly and the ungodly. The great Goethe, whose Walpurgis Night "He-Apes" made Elia put out his tongue, read, we learn, with no little pleasure some fantastic skit of this incorrigible one. Did he discern—the sublime Olympian—what a cunning flute player lurked under the queer mask? "Something between a Jew, a Gentleman and an Angel" he liked to fancy he looked; and one must confess that in the subtlest of all senses of that word, a gentleman he was.

Lamb's "essays" were written at off hours, when he could escape from his office. Once completely freed from the necessity of office work, his writing lost its magic. His genius was of that peculiarly delicate texture which requires the stimulus of reaction. One cannot be too grateful that the incomparable Pater, after Lamb himself, perhaps, the greatest master of English prose, found it necessary to utter his appreciation. Pater, as usual, hits the mark with an infallible hand when he speaks of that overhanging Sophoclean tragedy which darkened Lamb's earlier days and never quite left him.

It is, of course, this, the sense of one living always on the edge of a precipice, that gives such piquancy and charm to Elia's mania for "little things." Well might he turn to "little things," when great things—his Sun and his Moon—had been turned for him to Blood! But, as Pater suggests, there is "Philosophy" in all this, and more Philosophy than many suppose. It is unfortunate that the unworldly Coleridge and the worldly Thackeray should

CHARLES LAMB

have both pitched upon Lamb's "saintliness" to make copy of. Nothing infuriated him more than such a tone towards himself. And he was right to be infuriated. His "unselfishness," his "sweetness," of which these good men make so much, were only one aspect of the Philosophy of his whole life. Lamb was, in his life, a great epicurean philosopher, as, in all probability, many other "saints" have been. The things in him that fretted Carlyle, his fits of intoxication, his outbursts of capricious impishness, his perversity and his irony, were just as much part of the whole scheme as were his celibacy and his relation to his sister.

What one can really gather from Lamb is nothing less than a very wise and very subtle "way of life," a way that, amid many outrageous experiences, will be found singularly lucky.

In the first place, let it be noted, Lamb deliberately cultivates the art of "transforming the commonplace." It is as absurd to deny the existence of this element—from which we all suffer—as it is to maintain that it cannot be changed. It *can* be changed. That is precisely what this kind of rare genius does. It is a miracle, of course, but everything in art is a miracle.

Nature tosses out indiscriminately her motley productions, and if you are born for such "universalism," you may swallow them wholesale. The danger of such a downright manner of going to work is that it blunts one's critical sense. If you swallow everything just as it is, you *taste* very little. But Charles Lamb is nothing if not "critical," nothing if not an Epicure, and his manner of dealing with the "commonplace" sharpens rather than blunts the edge of one's taste.

And what is this manner? It is nothing less than an indescribable blending of Christianity and Paganism. Heine, another of Carlyle's "blackguards," achieves the same synthesis. It is this spiritual achievement—at once a religious and an aesthetic triumph—that makes Elia, for all his weaknesses, such a really great man. The Wordsworths and Coleridges who patronized him were too self-opiniated and individualistic to be able to enter into either tradition.

Wordsworth is neither a Christian or a Pagan. He is a moral philosopher. Elia is an artist, who understands the *importance of ritual* in life—but of naturalness in ritual.

How difficult, whether as a thinker or a man, is it to be natural in one's loves and hates! How many quite authoritative Philistines never really let the world know how Bohemian at heart they are! And how much of our modern "artistic feeling" is a pure affectation! Now, whatever Elia was not, he was wantonly, wickedly, whimsically natural.

He never concealed his religious feelings,

his superstitious feelings. He never concealed his fancies, his fads, his manias, his vices. He never concealed his emotion when he felt a thrill of passionate faith. He never concealed it when he felt a thrill of blasphemous doubt.

He accepted life's little pleasures as they appeared, and did not hesitate to make "cults" of the ones that appeared most appealing. If he had Philistine feelings, he indulged them without shame. If he had recondite and "artistic" feelings, he indulged them also without shame. He is one of the few great men not afraid to be un-original, and hence he is the most original of all. "I cannot," says he, "sit and think. Books think for me." Well, books did "think for him," for he managed to press the books of the great poets into his service, as no mortal writer has ever dared to do before. And he could do it without impairing his originality, because he was as original as the great poets he used. We say deliberately "poets," for, as Pater points out, to find Lamb's rivals in sheer imaginative genius, we have to leave the company of those who write prose.

Do the humorous ecclesiastics and scholarly tutors who profess to understand Elia ever peep into that Essay called "Witches," or that other Essay called "A Child-Angel"? There are things here that are written for a very different circle. Certain sentences in "Dream-children," too, have a beauty that takes a natural man's breath completely away. Touches of far-off romance, terrible and wistful as "anonymous ballads," alternate with gestures of Rabelaisian humour, such as generous souls love. Elia's style is the only thing in English prose that can be called absolutely perfect. Compared with the rich, capricious, wilful, lingering by the way of Lamb's manner, Pater's is precise, demure and over-grave, Wilde's fantastic and over-provocative, Ruskin's intolerably rhetorical.

Into what other prose style could the magic of Shakespeare's "little touches" be drawn, or the high melancholy of Milton's imagery be led, without producing a frightful sense of the incongruous? He can quote them both—or any other great old master—and if it were not for the "inverted commas" we should not be aware of the insertion.

Elia cannot say anything, not the simplest thing, without giving it a turn, a twist, a lift, a lightness, a grace, that would redeem the very grease-spots on a scullion's apron!

There is no style in the world like it. Germany, France, Italy, Russia have no Charles Lamb. Their Flauberts and D'Annunzios belong to a different tribe. Even Turgenieff, just because he has to "get on with his story," cannot do precisely this.

Every single one of the "essays" and most of the "letters" can be read over and over again, and their cadences caressed as if they were living people's features. And they are living. They are as living as those Japanese Prints so maddening to some among us, or as the drawings of Lionardo. They also—in their place—are "pure line," to use the ardent modern slang, and unpolluted "imaginative suggestion."

The mistake our "aesthetes" made, these lovers of Egyptian dancers and Babylonian masks, is that they suppose the simplicity of Lamb's subjects debar him from the rare effects. Ah! They little know! He can take the wistfulness of children, and the quaint gestures of dead Comedians, and the fantasies of old worm-eaten folios, and the shadows of sun-dials upon cloistered lawns, and the heart-breaking evasions of such as "can never know love," and out of these things he can make a music as piteous and lovely as Ophelia's songs. It is a curious indication of the lack of real poetic feeling in the feverish art-neophytes of our age that they should miss these things in Elia. One wonders if they have ever felt the remote translunar beauty that common faces and old, dim, pitiful things can wear sometimes. It would seem not. Like Herod the Tetrarch, they must have "Peacocks whose crying calls the rain, and the spreading of their tails brings down the Moon;" they must have "opals that burn with flame as cold as ice," and onyxes and amber and the tapestries of Tyre. The pansies that "are for thoughts" touch them not and the voices of the street-singers leave them cold.

It is precisely the lack of natural kindly humour in these people, who must always be clutching "cameos from Syracuse" between their fingers, which leads them, when the tension of the "gem-like flame" can be borne no more, into sheer garishness and brutality. One knows it so well, that particular tone; the tone of the jaded amorist, for whom "the unspeakable rural solitudes" and "the sweet security of streets" mean, both of them, boredom and desolation.

It is not their subtlety that makes them thus suffer; it is their lack of it. What? Is the poignant world-old play of poor mortal men and women, with their absurdities and excesses, their grotesque reserves and fantastic confessions, their advances and withdrawals, not *interesting* enough to serve? It serves sufficiently; it serves well enough, when genius takes it in hand. Perhaps, after all, it is *that* which is lacking.

Charles Lamb went through the world with many avoidances, but one thing he did not avoid—the innocence of unmitigated foolishness! He was able to give to the Simple Simons of this life that Rabelaisian touch of magnanimous understanding which makes

CHARLES LAMB

even the leanest wits among us glow. He went through the world with strange timidities and no daring stride. He loitered in its by-alleys. He drifted through its Bazaars. He sat with the crowd in its Circuses. He lingered outside its churches. He ate his "pot of honey" among its graves. And as he went his way, irritable and freakish, wayward and arbitrary, he came, by chance, upon just those side-lights and intimations, those rumours and whispers, those figures traced on sand and dust and water, which, more than all the Law and the Prophets, draw near to the unuttered word.

DICKENS

DICKENS

T is absurd, of course, to think that it is necessary to "hold a brief" for Dickens. But sometimes, when one comes across charming and exquisite people who "cannot read him," one is tempted to give one's personal appreciation that kind of form.

Dickens is one of the great artists of the world, and he is so, in spite of the fact that in certain spheres, in the sphere of Sex, for instance, or the sphere of Philosophy, he is such a hopeless conventionalist. It is because we are at this hour so preoccupied with Sex, in our desire to readjust the conventions of Society and Morality towards it, that a great artist, who simply leaves it out altogether, or treats it with a mixture of the conventionality of the preacher and the worst foolishness of the crowd, is an artist whose appeal is seriously handicapped.

Yet, given this "lacuna," this amazing "gap" in his work, a deprivation much more serious than his want of "philosophy," Dickens is a writer of colossal genius, whose originality and vision puts all our modern "literateurs" to shame. One feels this directly one opens any volume of his. Only a great creative genius could so dominate, for instance, his mere "illustrators," as to mesmerize them completely into his manner. And certainly his illustrators are *drugged* with the Dickens atmosphere. Those hideous-lovely persons, whose legs and arms are so thin that it is impossible to suppose they ever removed their clothes; do they not strut and leer and ogle and grin and stagger and weep, in the very style of their author?

Remembering my "brief," and the sort of jury, among my friends, I have to persuade, I am not inclined in this sketch to launch out into panegyrics upon Mr. Micawber and Mrs. Gamp and Mr. Pecksniff and Betsy Trotwood and Bill Sikes and Dick Swiveller and Bob Sawyer and Sam Weller and Mark Tapley and Old Scrooge. The mere mention of these names, which, to some, would suggest the music of the spheres, to others would suggest forced merriment, horrible Early Victorian sentiment, and that sort of hackneyed "unction" of sly moral elders, which is youth's especial Hell. Much wiser were it, as it seems to me, to indicate what in Dickens—in his style, his method, his vision, his art—actually appeals to one particular mind. I think it is to be found in his childlike Imagination. Now,

DICKENS

the modern cult for children has reached such fantastic limits that one has to be very careful when one uses that word. But Dickens is childlike, not as Oscar Wilde—that Uranian Baby—or as Paul Verlaine—that little "pet lamb" of God—felt themselves to be childlike, or as the artificial-minded Robert Louis Stevenson fooled his followers into thinking him. He is really and truly childlike. His imagination and vision are literally the imagination and vision of children. We have not all played at Pirates and Buccaneers. We have not all dreamed of Treasure-Islands and Marooned sailors. We have not all "believed in Fairies." These rather tiresome and over-rung-upon aspects of children's fancies are, after all, very often nothing more than middle-aged people's damned affectations. The children's cult at the present day plays strange tricks.

But Dickens, from beginning to end, has the real touch, the authentic reaction. How should actual and living children, persecuted by "New Educational Methods," glutted with toys, depraved by "understanding sympathy," and worn out by performances of "Peter Pan," believe—really and truly—in fairies any more? But, in spite of sentimental Child-worshippers, let us not hesitate to whisper: "It doesn't matter in the least if they don't!" The "enlightened" and cultivated mothers, who grow unhappy when they find their darlings cold to Titania and Oberon and to the more "poetic" modern fairies, with the funny names, may rest in peace. If the house they inhabit and the street they inhabit be not sanitarized and art-decorated beyond all human interest, they may let their little ones alone. They will dream their dreams. They will invent their games. They will talk to their shadows. They will blow kisses to the Moon. And all will go well with "the Child in the House," even if he has not so much as even heard of "the Blue Bird"!

If these uncomfortably "childlike" people read Dickens, they would know how a child really does regard life, and perhaps they would be a little shocked. For it is by no means only the "romantic" and "aesthetic" side of things that appeals to children. They have their nightmares, poor imps, and such devils follow them as older people never dream of. Dickens knew all that, and in his books the thrill of the supernatural, as it hovers over chairs and tables and pots and pans, is never far away. It lurks, that repelling-alluring Terror, in a thousand simple places. It moves in the darkness of very modern cupboards. It hides in the recesses of very modern cellars. It pounces out from the eaves of quite modern attics. It is there, halfway up the Staircase.

DICKENS

It is there, halfway down the Passage. And God knows whither it comes or where it goes!

To endow the little every-day objects that surround us—a certain picture in a certain light, a certain clock or stove in a certain shadow, a certain corner of the curtain when the wind moves it—with the fetish-magic of natural "animism"; that is the real childlike trick, and that is what Dickens does. It is, of course, something not confined to people who are children in years. It is the old, sweet Witch-Hag, Mystery, that, sooner or later, has us all by the throat!

And that is why, to me, Dickens is so great a writer. Since men have come to live so much in cities; since houses and streets and rooms and passages and windows and basements have come to mean more to them than fields and woods, it is essential that "the Old Man covered with a Mantle," the Ancient of Ancients, the Disturber of Rational Dreams, should move into the town, too, and mutter and murmur in its shadows!

How hard a thing is it, to put into words the strange attraction and the strange terror which the dwellings of mortal men have the power of exciting! To drift at nightfall into an unknown town, and wander through its less frequented ways, and peep into its dark, empty churches, and listen to the wind in the stunted trees that grow by its Prison, and watch some flickering particular light high up in some tall house—the light of a harlot, a priest, an artist, a murderer—surely there is no imaginative experience equal to this! Then, the things one sees, by chance, by accident, through half-open doors and shutter-chinks and behind lifted curtains! Verily the ways of men upon earth are past finding out, and their madness beyond interpretation!

It is not only children—and yet it is children most of all—who get the sense, in a weird, sudden flash, of the demonic life of inanimate things. Why are our houses so full of things that one had better not look at, things that, like the face of Salome, had better be seen in mirrors, and things that must be forbidden to look at us? The houses of mortal men are strange places. They are sepulchres and cemeteries. Dungeons are they, and prison cells. Not one of them but have murderous feet going up and down. Not one of them but have ravisher's hands, fumbling, back and forth, along the walls. For the secret wishes, and starved desires, and mad cravings, and furious revolts, of the hearts of men and women, living together decently in their "homes," grow by degrees palpable and real and gather to themselves strange shapes.

No writer who has ever lived can touch Dickens in indicating this sort of familiar sorcery and the secret of its terror. For it is children, more than any, who are conscious how "haunted" all manner of places and things are. And people themselves! The searching psychologists are led singularly astray. They peer and pry and repine, and all the while the real essence of the figure lies in its momentary expression—in its most superficial gesture.

Dickens' world is a world of gnomes and hob-goblins, of ghouls and of laughing angels. The realist of the Thackeray School finds nothing but monstrous exaggeration here—and fantastic mummery. If he were right, pardieu! If his sleek "reality" were all that there was—"alarum!" We were indeed "betrayed"! But no; the children are right. Dickens is right. Neither "realist" or "psychologist" hits the mark, when it comes to the true diablerie of living people. There is something more whimsical, more capricious, more *unreal*, than philosophers suppose about this human pantomime. People are actually—as every child knows—much worse and much better than they "ought" to be. And, as every child knows, too, they tune their souls up to the pitch of their "masks." The surface of things is the heart of things; and the protruded goblin-tongue, the wagged head, the groping fingers, the shuffling step, are just as significant of the mad play-motif as any hidden thoughts. People *think* with their bodies, and their looks and gestures; nay! their very garments are words, tones, whispers, in their general Confession.

The world of Dickens' fantastic creations is all the nearer to the truth of our life because it is so arbitrary and "impossible." He seems to go backwards and forwards with a torch, throwing knobs, jags, wrinkles, corrugations, protuberancies, cavities, horns, and snouts into terrifying illumination. But we are like that! That is what we actually are. That is how the Pillar of Fire sees us. Then, again, are we to limit our interest, as these modern writers do, to the beautiful people or the interesting people or the gross, emphatic people. Dickens is never more childlike than when he draws us, wonderingly and confidingly, to the stark knees of a Mrs. Pipchin, or when he drives us away, in unaccountable panic-terror, from the rattling jet-beads of a Miss Murdstone.

Think of the vast, queer, dim-lighted world wherein live and move all those funny, dusty, attenuated, heart-breaking figures, of such as wear the form of women—and yet may never know "love"! It is wonderful—when you think of it—how much of absorbing interest is left in life, when you have eliminated "sex," suppressed "psychology," and left philosophy out! Then appear all those queer attractions and repulsions which are purely superficial, and even material, and yet which are so dominant. Mother of God! How unnecessary to bring in Fairies and Blue Birds, when the solemnity of some little seamstress and her sorceress hands, and the quaint knotting of her poor wisp of hair, would be enough to keep a child staring and dreaming for hours upon hours!

Life in a great city is like life in an enchanted forest. One never knows what hideous ogre or what exquisite hamadryad one may encounter. And the little ways of all one's scrabbling and burrowing and chuckling and nodding and winking house-mates! To go through the world expecting adventures is to find them sooner or later. But one need only cross one's threshold to find one adventure—the adventure of a new, unknown fellow-creature, full of suspicion, full of cloudy malice, full of secretive dreams, and yet ready to respond—poor devil—to a certain kind of signal!

Long reading of Dickens' books, like long living with children, gives one a wholesome dread of cynicism and flippancy. Children's games are more serious than young men's love-affairs, and they must be treated so. It is not exactly that life is to be "taken seriously." It is to be taken for what it is—an extraordinary Pantomime. The people who will not laugh with Pierrot because his jokes are so silly, and the people who will not cry with Columbine because her legs are so thin, may be shrewd psychologists and fastidious artists—but, God help them! they are not in the game.

The romance of city-life is one thing. The romance of a particular city leads us further. Dickens has managed to get the inner identity of London; what is permanent in it; what can be found nowhere else; as not even Balzac got hold of Paris. London is terrible and ghastly. One knows that; but the wretchedest of its "gamins" knows that it is something else also. More than any place on earth it seems to have that weight, that mass, that depth, that foursquare solidity, which reassures and comforts, in the midst of the illusions of life. It descends so far, with its huge human foundations, that it gives one the impression of a monstrous concrete Base, sunk into eternity, upon which, for all its accummulated litter and débris, man will be able to build, perhaps has begun already, to build, his Urbs Beata. And Dickens entered with dramatic clairvoyance into every secret of this Titanic mystery. He knew its wharfs, its bridges, its viaducts, its alleys, its dens, its parks, its squares, its churches, its morgues, its circuses, its prisons, its hospitals, and its mad-houses. And as the human atoms of that fantastic, gesticulating, weeping, grinning crowd of his dance their crazy "Carmagnole," we cannot but feel that somehow we *must* gather strength and friendliness enough to applaud such a tremendous Performance.

Dickens was too great a genius to confine his demonic touch to the town alone. There are *suggestions* of his, relating to country roads and country Inns and country solitudes, like nothing else, except, perhaps, the Vignettes of Berwick. He carries the same "animism" into this also. And he notes and records sensations of the most evasive kind. The peculiar terror we feel, for instance, mixed with a sort of mad pity, when by chance we light upon some twisted root-trunk, to which the shadows have given outstretched arms. The vague feelings, too, so absolutely unaccountable, that the sight of a lonely gate, or weir, or park-railing, or sign-post, or ruined shed, or tumble-down sheep-fold, may suddenly arouse, when we feel that in some weird manner we are the accomplices of the Thing's tragedy, are feelings that Dickens alone among writers seems to understand. A road with no people upon it, and the wind alone sobbing there; with blind eyes and wrinkled forehead; a pool by the edge of a wide marsh-land—like the marsh-land in "Great Expectations"—with I know not what reflected in it, and waiting, always waiting, for something that does not come; a low, bent, knotted pine-tree, over which the ravens fly, one by one, shrieking; these are the things that to some people—to children, for instance—remain in the mind when all else of their country journey is forgotten.

There is no one but Dickens who has a style that can drag these things into light. His style shrieks sometimes like a ghoul tugging at the roots of a mandrake. At other times it wails like a lost soul. At other times it mutters, and whimpers, and pipes in its throat, like an old man blinking at the moon. At other times it roars and thunders like ten thousand drunken devils. At other times it breaks into wistful, tender, little-girl sobs—and catches the rhythm of poetry—as in the death of Nell. Sometimes a character in Dickens will say something so humorously pregnant, so directly from what we hear in street and tavern, that art itself "gives up," and applauds, speechless.

After all, it is meet and right that there should be one great author, undistracted by psychology—unseduced by eroticism. There remain a few quite important things to deal with, when these are removed! Birth, for instance—the mystery of birth—and the mystery of death. One never forgets death in reading Dickens. He has a thought, a pity, for those things that once were men and women, lying, with their six feet of earth upon them, in our English Churchyards, so horribly still, while the mask of their sorrow yields to the yet more terrible grin of our mortality's last jest.

And to the last he is—like all children—the lover of Players. Every poor dog of Public Entertainer, from the Barrel-Organ man to him who pulls the ropes for Punch and Judy, has his unqualified devotion. The modern Stage may see strange revolutions, some of them by no means suitable to children—but we need not be alarmed. There will always remain the larger Stage, the stage of man's own Exits and Entrances; and there, at any rate, while Dickens is their "Manager," Pierrot may weep and dance, and Pierrette dance and weep, knowing that they will not be long without their audience, or long without their applause!

He was a vulgar writer. Why not? England would not be England—and what would London be?—if we didn't have a touch, a smack, a sprinkling of that ingredient!

He was a shameless sentimentalist. Why not? It is better to cry than to comb one's hair all day with an ivory comb.

He was a monstrous melodramatist. Why not? To be born is a melodrama. To play "hide-and-seek" with Death is a melodrama. And some have found melodramatic satisfaction in letting themselves be caught. All the World's a Puppet-Show, and if the Big Showman jerks his wires so extravagantly, why should not the Little Showman do the same?

GOETHE

GOETHE

HAS the enigmatic wisdom of Goethe been exhausted—after these years —and after the sudden transits across our sky of more flashing meteors? Ah! I deem not yet. Still he holds the entrance to the mysterious Gate, over the portals of which is written, not "Lasciate ogni speranza!" but "Think of Living!" A thunder-rifted heart he bears, but victory, not defeat, looks forth from his wide, outward-gazing eyes! One hand holds the Skull, engraved with all the secret symbols of man's ascent out of the bosom of Nature; engraved, yes!—by all the cunningest tools of Science and her unwearied research; but the other, raised aloft, noble and welcoming, carries the laurel crown of the triumph of Imagination!

So, between Truth and Poetry—"im ganzen guten, schonen,"—stands our Lord of Life!

Exhausted, the wisdom of Goethe? Ah, no! —hardly fathomed yet, in its uppermost levels!

If it were really possible to put into words the whole complex world of impressions and visions, of secrets and methods, which that name suggests, one would be a wiser disciple than Eckermann. Fragment by fragment, morsel by morsel, the great Figure limns itself against the shadow of the years.

Is it too presumptuous a task to seek to evoke—taking first one impression of him and then another, first one reaction and then another—what this mysterious Name has come to mean for us? One hears the word "cosmic" whispered. It is whispered too often in these days. But "cosmic," with its Whitmanesque, modern connotation, does not exactly fit Goethe. Goethe did not often abandon himself in Dionysian fury to the ultimate Elements. When he did—in his earlier youth—before the hardening process of his Italian Journey had sealed his protection from such romantic lapses —it was not quite in the strained, desperate, modern manner. One feels certain, thinking of what he was, at Frankfurt, at Leipsig, at Strassburg, at Weimar, that he always kept a clear, cool, Apollonian head, mad and amorous though his escapades may seem!

I do not fancy that ever once did Goethe really "give himself away," or lose the four-square solidity of his balance in any wild staggering to left or right. No; the Goethean temper, the Goethean attitude, cannot be described as "cosmic," while that word implies a certain complete yielding to a vague earth-worship. There was nothing vague about Goethe's *in-*

timacy, if I may put it so, with the Earth. He and It seemed destined to understand one another most *serenely,* in a shrewd and deliberate conspiracy!

The Goethean attitude to the Universe is too self-poised and self-centered to be adequately rendered by any word that suggests complete abandonment. It is too—what shall I say?—too sly and *demonic*—too much *inside* the little secrets of the great Mother—to be summed up in a word that suggests a sort of Titanic whirlwind of embraces. And yet, on the other hand, it is quite as easy to exaggerate the Olympian aspect of Goethe. When this is carried too far, something in him, something extraordinarily characteristic, evaporates, like a thin stream of Parnassian smoke.

How shall I express what this is? Perhaps it is the *German* in him. For, in spite of all Nietzsche's Mediterraneanizing of this Superman, Goethe was profoundly and inveterately German. The Rhine-Maidens rocked him in his cradle and, though he might journey to Rome or Troy or Carthage, it was to the Rhine-Maidens that he returned. Yes, I do not think that those understand him best who keep bowing to the ground and muttering "Olympian"!

Am I carrying this particular taper-light of discrimination too far when I say that there is, to the Celtic mind at least, something humorously naive and childlike in Goethe, mixed in, queerly enough, with all his rich, mellow, and even worldly, wisdom? One overtakes him, now and then, and catches him, as it were, off his guard, in little pathetic lapses into a curious simplicity—a simplicity grave-eyed, potentious and solemn—almost like that of some great Infant-Faun, trying very seriously to learn the difficult syllables of our human "Categorical Imperative"! World-child, as he was, the magic of the universe pouring through him, one sometimes feels a strange, dim hope with regard to that dubious general Issue, when we find him so confident about the presence of the mysterious Being he worshipped; and so transparently certain of his personal survival after Death!

There is no one, except Leonardo Da Vinci, in the whole history of our Planet, who gives us quite that sense of a person possessed of some secret illumination not granted to the rest of the world. There is much reassurance in this. More than has been, perhaps, realized. For it is probable that "in his caves of ice," Leonardo also felt himself indestructible by the Arch-Enemy. One thinks of those Cabbalistic words of old Glanville, "Man does not yield himself to Death—save by the weakness of his mortal Will."

Goethe collecting fossils and crystals and specimens of rock-strata; Goethe visiting Botanical Gardens and pondering on the Metamorphosis of Plants; Goethe climbing Strassburg Cathedral-Spire; Goethe meeting the Phantom of Himself as he returned from the arms of Frederika; Goethe "experiencing the sensation" of crossing the "Firing-Line"; Goethe "announcing" to Eckermann that that worthy man had better avoid undertaking any "great" literary work; Goethe sending Frau von Stein sausages from his breakfast-table; Goethe consoling himself in the Storm by observing his birth-star Lucifer, and thinking of the Lake of Galilee, are pictures of noble and humorous memory which reconcile one to the Comedy of Living!

How vividly returns to me—your pardon, reader!—the first time I read "The Sorrows of Werter" in that little "Three-penny" edition published by Messrs. Cassell! It was in a Barge, towed by three Horses, on the River, between Langport and Bridgewater, in the County of Somerset! The majority of the company were as rowdy a set of good-humored Bean-Feasters as ever drank thin beer in a ramshackle tavern. But there was one of them —this is twenty-five years ago, reader!—a girl as fragile as a peeled Willow-wand—and teased by the rude badinage of our companions we sheltered—as the friendly mists rose—under a great Tarpaulin at the barge's stern. Where is that girl now, I wonder? Is she alive? Will she ever blush with anger at being thus gently lifted up, from beneath the kind Somersetshire mists, into an hour's publicity? Who can tell? We are all passing one another, in mist-darkened barges, swift or slow. She is a wraith, a shadow, a receding phantom; but I wave my hand to her over the years! I shall always associate her with Lotte; and I never smell the peculiar smell of Tarpaulin without thinking of "the Sorrows of Werter."

"Werter" has certainly the very droop and bewilderment of youth's first passion. It is good to plunge one's hands, when one has grown cynical and old, into that innocent, if somewhat turbid, fountain. When we pass to "Wilhelm Meister," we are in quite a different world. The earlier part of this book has the very stamp of the Goethean "truth and poetry." One can read it side by side with the great "Autobiography" and find the shrewd insight and oracular wisdom quite equally convincing in the invention and the reality. What an unmistakable and unique character all these imaginary persons of Goethe's stories have! They are so different from any other persons in fiction! Wherein does the difference lie? It is hard to say. In a sense, they are more life-like and real. In another sense, they are more fantastic. Sometimes they seem mere dolls—like the figures in his own puppet-show—and we can literally "see the puppets dallying."

Jarno is a queer companion for a man to

have. And what of the lady who, when she was asked whether she had ever loved, answered, "never or always"? Phillina is a very loving and an extremely vivacious wench. Goethe's sublime unconsciousness of ordinary moral qualms is never better observed than in the story of this extravagant young minx. Then, in the midst of it all, the arresting, ambiguous little figure of poor Mignon! What does she do—a child of pure lyrical poetry—a thing out of the old ballads—in this queer, grave, indecent company? That elaborate description of Mignon's funeral so carefully arranged by the Aesthetic "Uncle," has it not all the curious qualities of the Goethean vein—its clairvoyant insight into the under-truth of Nature—its cold-blooded pre-occupation with "Art"—its gentle irony—its mania for exact detail? The "gentle irony" of which I speak has its opportunity in the account of the "Beautiful Soul" or "Fair Saint." It reads, in places, like the tender dissection of a lovely corpse by a genial, elderly Doctor.

But the passage which, for me, is most precious is that Apprentice's "Indenture." I suppose in no other single paragraph of human prose is there so much concentrated wisdom. "To act is easy—to think is hard!" How extraordinarily true that is! But it is not the precise tune of the strenuous preachers of our time! The whole idea of the "Pedagogic Province," ruled over by that admirable Abbé, is so exquisitely in Goethe's most wise and yet most simple manner! The passage about the "Three Reverences" and the "Creed" is as good an instance of that sublime Spinozistic way of dealing with the current religion as that amazing remark he made once to Eckerman about his own faith: "When I want scientific unity, I am a Pantheist. When I desire poetical multifariousness, I am a Polytheist. And when my moral nature requires a Personal God—*there is room for That also!*"

When one comes to speak of Faust, it is necessary for us to remember the words the great man himself used to his follower in speaking of this masterpiece. Eckermann teased him for interpretations. "What," said he to Goethe, "is the leading Idea in the Poem?" "Do you suppose," answered the Sage, "that a thing into which I have put the Life-Blood of all my days is able to be summoned up in anything so narrow and limited as an Idea?"

Personally, I do not hesitate to say that I think Faust is the most permanently *interesting* of all the works that have proceeded from the human brain.

Its attitude to life is one which ultimately has more to strengthen and sustain and put courage—if not the Devil—into us than anything I know. When I meet a man who shall tell me that the Philosophy of his life is the Philosophy of Faust, I bow down humbly before him. I did meet such a man once. I think he was a Commercial Traveller from Buffalo.

How wisely Goethe deals in Faust with the problem—if it be a problem—of Evil! His suggestion seems to be that the spirit of Evil in the world—"part of that Nothing out of which came the All"—plays an absolutely essential role. "By means of it God fulfils his most cherished purposes." Had Faust not seduced poor little Gretchen, he would never have passed as far as he did along the road of Initiation, and the spirit of his Victim—in her translunar Apotheosis—would not have been *there* to lift him Heavenwards at the last. And yet no one could say that Goethe disparages the enormity of Faust's crime. That ineffable retort of Mephistopheles, when, on those "black horses," they are whirled through the night to her dungeon, "She is not the first," has the essence of all pity and wrath in its cruel sting. Mephistopheles himself is the most interesting of all Devils. And he is so because, although he knows perfectly well—queer Son of Chaos as he is—that he is bound to be defeated, he yet goes on upon his evil way, and continues to resist the great stream of Life which, according to his view, had better never have broken loose from primeval Nothingness.

That is ultimately Goethe's contribution to

the disputes about what we call "God." The name does not matter. "Feeling is all in all. The name is sound and smoke." "God," or "the Good," is to Goethe simply the eternal stream of life, working slowly upwards, onwards, to unknown goals. All that opposes itself to this Life-stream is evil. Morality, a man-made local convention, is our present blundering method of assisting this great Force, and preventing its sterility, or dissipation. In his conception of the nature of this Life-stream Goethe is more Catholic and more subtle than Nietzsche.

Self-realization? Certainly! That is an aspect of it which was not likely to be forgotten by the great Egoist whose sole object, as he confessed, was to "build up the Pyramid of his Existence" from the broadest possible base. But not only self-realization. The "dying to live" of the Christian, as well as "the rising above one's body" of the Platonist, have their part there. Asceticism itself, with all its degrees of passionate or philosophical purity, is as much an evocation of the world-spirit—of the essential nature of the System of Things—as is the other.

It is, of course, ultimately, quite a mad hope to desire to *convert* "the Spirit that Denies." He, too, under the Lord, is an accomplice of the Life-stream. He helps it forward, even while he opposes himself to it, just as a bulwark of submerged rocks make the tide leap landward with more foaming fury!

Goethe's idea of the "Eternal Feminine" leading us "upward and on" is not at all the sentimental nonsense which Nietzsche fancied it. In a profound sense it is absolutely true. Nor need the more anti-feminist among us be troubled by such a Truth. We have just seen that the Devil himself is a means, and a very essential means, for leading us "upward and on."

Goethe is perfectly right. The "love of women," though a destructive force, and a frightful force as far as certain kinds of "art" and "philosophy" are concerned, cannot be looked upon as anything but "a provocation to creation," when the whole large scheme of existence is taken into account.

I think myself that it is easy to make too much of Goethe's Pantheism. The Being he worshipped was simply "Whatever Mystery" lies behind the ocean of Life. And if no "mystery" lies behind the ocean of life,—very well! A Goethean disciple is able, then, to worship Life, with no mystery behind it! It is rather the custom among clever, tiresome people to disparage that *second part of Faust,* with its world-panoramic procession of all the gods and demi-gods and angels and demons that have ever visited this earth. I do not disparage it. I have never found it dull. Dull would he be, as "the fat weed that rots itself in case on Lethe's wharf," who found nothing curious and provocative about these Sirens and Centaurs and Lemures and Larvae and Cabiri and Phorkyads! I can myself endure very pleasantly even the society of those "Blessed Boys" which some have found so distressing. As for the Devil, in the end, making "indecent overtures" to the little Heavenly Butterflies, who pelt him with roses—even that does not confuse my mind or distract my senses. It is the "other side of the Moon"—the under-mask of the world-comedy, and the incidental "saving" of Dr. Faust is not more essential in the great mad game!

Read Faust, both portions of it, dear reader, and see if you do not feel, with me, that, in the last resort, one leaves this rich, strange poem with a nobler courage to endure life, and a larger view of its amazing possibilities!

I wonder if that curious novel of Goethe's called the "Elective Affinities" is perused as widely as it deserves? That extraordinary company of people! And the patient, portentious interest Goethe compels us to take in the laying out of gardens and the beautifying of church-yards! "The Captain," "the Architect"—not to speak of the two bewildering women—do they not suggest fantastic figures out of one's memories of remotest childhood? I suppose to a world-child like Goethe, watching, with grave super-human interest, all our little pre-occupations, we have all of us something of the sweet pedantry of these people—we are all of us "Captains" and "Architects" with some odd twist in our quiet heads.

The solemn immorality, amounting to outrageous indecency, of those scenes between the assorted lovers when they make "double" love, and behind the mask of their legitimate attachments follow their "elective affinities," is a thing that may well stagger the puritan reader. The puritan reader will, indeed, like old Carlyle, be tempted more than once to fling these grave, unblushing chronicles, with their deep, oracular wisdom and their shameless details, into the dust-heap. But it were wiser to refrain. After all, one cannot conceal from one's self that things are *like that*—and if the hyaena's howl, from the filthy marshes of earth's weird edge and the thick saliva on his oozing jaws, nauseates our preciosity, and besmirches our self-esteem, we must remember that this is the way the Lord of "the Prologue in Heaven" has willed that the scavengers of life's cesspools go about their work!

Probably it will not be the "indecency" of certain things in Goethe that will most offend our modern taste; it will be that curious, grave pre-occupation of his, so objective and stiff, with artistic details, and architectural details, and theatrical details!

One must remember his noble saying, "Earnestness alone makes life Eternity," and that other "saying" about Art having, as its main purpose, the turning of the "Transitory" into the "Permanent"! If the Transitory is really to be turned into the Permanent, we must take ourselves and our work very seriously indeed!

And such "seriousness," such high, patient, unwearied seriousness, is, after all, Goethe's bequest to our flippant and fanciful generation. He knows well enough our deepest doubt, our most harrowing scepticism. He has long ago "been through all that." But he has "returned"—not exactly like Nietzsche, with a fierce, scornful, dramatic cry, to a contemptuous "superficiality"—he has returned to the actual possibilities that the world offers, "superficial" and otherwise, of turning the whole strange business into a solid, four-square "work of art." We must reject "evil," quietly and ironically; not because it is condemned by human morality, but because "we have our work to do"! We must live in "the good" and "the true," not because it is our "duty" so to do, but because only along this particular line does the "energy without agitation" of the "abysmal mothers" communicate itself to our labour.

And so we come back, like the grief-stricken children over Mignon's grave, to Life and Life's toil. There only, in the inflexible development of what taste, of what discernment, of what power, of what method, of what demonic genius, we may have been granted by the gods, lies "the cosmic secret." That is all we have in our human hands, that malleable stuff out of which Fate made us—and only in the shrewd, unwearied use of that shall we prove our love to the Being "who cannot love us in return," and make our illusion of Free-Will part of his universal Purpose!

MATTHEW ARNOLD

MATTHEW ARNOLD

T is easy to miss the especial grandeur of Matthew Arnold's work. The airy persiflage of his prose—its reiterated lucidities—pleasing to some, irritating to others, will have a place, but not a very important place, in English Literature. Even those magical and penetrating "aphorisms" with which he has held the door open to so many religious and moral vistas tease us a little now, and—suggestive enough in their hour—do not deepen and deepen upon the intellect with the weight of "aphorisms" from Epictetus or Goethe.

The "stream of tendency that makes for righteousness" runs a little shallow, and it has so many pebbles under its clear wave! That word of his, "the Secret of Jesus," wears best of all. It was a happy thought to use the word "secret"—a thought upon which those whose religious creed binds them to "the method" rather than "the secret," may well ponder!

As a critic, too, though illuminating and reassuring, he is far from clairvoyant. A quaint vein of pure, good-tempered, ethical *Philistin-*

ism prevents his really entering the evasive souls of Shelley or Keats or Heine. With Wordsworth or Byron he is more at home. But he misses many subtleties, even in their simple temperaments. He is no Proteus, no Wizard of critical metempsychosis. For all his airy wit, he is "a plain, blunt man, who loves his friend." In fact, when one compares him, as a sheer illuminator of psychological twilights, to Walter Pater, one realizes at once how easily a quite great man may "render himself stupid" by sprinkling himself with the holy water of Fixed Principles!

No, it is neither of Arnold, the Theological Free-Lance, or of Arnold, the Critic of Literature, that I want to speak, but of Arnold, the Poet.

Personally I hold the opinion that he was a greater poet than either Tennyson or Browning. His philosophy is a far nobler, truer, and more permanent thing than theirs, and there are passages and single lines in his poetry which over-top, by enormous distances, anything that they achieved.

You ask me what the Philosophy of Matthew Arnold was? It is easy to answer that. It was the philosophy of all the very greatest among mortal men! In his poetry he passes completely out of the region of Theological argument, and his attitude to life is the attitude of Sophocles and Virgil and Montaigne and Cervantes and Shakespeare and Goethe. Those who read Matthew Arnold, and love him, know that his intellectual tone is the tone of those great classical writers, and his conclusions their conclusions.

He never mocks our pain with foolish, unfounded hopes and he never permits mad despair to paralyse him. He takes life as it is, and, as we all have to do, makes the best of its confusions. If we are here "as on a darkling plain, swept by confused alarms of struggle and flight, where ignorant armies clash by night," we can at least be "true to one another."

One wonders sometimes if it be properly understood by energetic teachers of youth that there is only one intellectual attitude towards life, only one philosophy, only one ultimate mood. This is that mood of "resignation," which, from Homer to Matthew Arnold, is alone adapted, in the long run, to the taste of our days upon earth.

The real elements of our situation have not altered in the remotest degree since Achilles dragged Hector round the walls of Troy.

Men and women still love and hate; still "enjoy the sun" and "live light in the Spring"; still "advance true friends and beat back dangerous foes"—and upon them the same Constellations look down; and upon them the same winds blow; and upon them the same Sphinx glides through the obscurity, with the same insoluble Question.

Nothing has really changed. The "river of time" may pass through various landscapes, but it is the same river, and, at the last, it brings to us, as "the banks fade dimmer away" and "the stars come out," "murmurs and scents" of the same infinite Sea. Yes, there is only one Philosophy, as Disraeli said, jesting; and Matthew Arnold, among the moderns, is the one who has been allowed to put it into his poetry. For though, before the "Flamantia Moenia" of the world's triple brass, we are fain to bow our heads inconsolably, there come those moments when, a hand laid in ours, we think we know "the hills whence our life flows"!

The flowing of the river of life—the washing of the waves of life—how well one recalls, from Arnold's broken and not always musical stanzas, references to that sound—to the sound so like the sound of those real sea-tides that "Sophocles, long ago, heard in the Aegaean," and listened, thinking of many things, as we listen and think of many things today!

"For we are all like swimmers in the Sea,
"Poised on the top of a huge wave of Fate,
"And whether it will lift us to the land
"Or whether it will bear us out to Sea,
"Back out to Sea, to the dark gulfs of Death,
"We know not—

MATTHEW ARNOLD

"Only the event will teach us, in its hour."
I sometimes think that a certain wonderful blending of realism and magic in Matthew Arnold's poetry has received but scant justice.

In "the Forsaken Merman," for instance, there are many stanzas that make you smell the salt-foam and imagine all that lies, hidden and strange, down there upon the glittering sand. That line,

"Where great whales go sailing by
Round the world for ever and aye,"

has a liberating power that may often recur, when one is, God knows, far enough from the spouting of any whale! And the whole poem has a wistful, haunting beauty that never grows tedious.

Matthew Arnold is a true classical poet. It is strictly in accordance with the authentic tradition to introduce those touches of light, quaint, playful, airy realism into the most solemn poetry. It is what Virgil, Catullus, Theocritus, Milton, Landor, all did. Some persons grow angry with him for a certain tone of half-gay, half-sad, allusive tenderness, when he speaks of Oxford and the country round Oxford. I do not think there is anything unpleasing in this. So did Catullus talk of Sirmio; Horace of his Farm; Milton of "Deva's wizard-stream"; Landor of Sorrento and Amalfi.

It is all of a piece with the "resignation" of

a philosophy which does not expect that this or that change of dwelling will ease our pain; of a philosophy that naturally loves to linger over familiar well-sides and roadways and meadow-paths and hillsides, over the places where we went together, when we "still had Thyrsis."

The direct Nature-poetry of Matthew Arnold, touching us with the true classic touch, and yet with something, I know not what, of more wistful tenderness added, is a great refreshment after the pseudo-magic, so vague and unsatisfying, of so much modern verse.

"It matters not. Light-cormer he has flown!
But we shall have him in the sweet spring days,
With whitening hedges and uncrumpling fern,
And blue-bells trembling by the forest ways,
And scent of hay new-mown—"

Or that description of the later season:

"Too quick despairer! Wherefore wilt thou go?
Soon will the high Midsummer pomps come on,
Soon shall we have gold-dusted Snapdragon,
Sweet-William with his homely cottage-smell,
And Stocks, in fragrant blow.
Roses that down the alleys shine afar,

MATTHEW ARNOLD

   And open Jasmin-muffled lattices,
   And groups under the dreaming garden-trees,
   And the pale Moon and the white Evening-Star."

True to the "only philosophy," Matthew Arnold is content to indicate how for each one of us the real drama of life goes on with a certain quite natural, quite homely, quite quiet background of the strip of earth where we first loved and dreamed, and were happy, and were sad, and knew loss and regret, and the limits of man's power to change his fate.

There is a large and noble calm about the poetry of this writer which has the effect upon one of the falling of cool water into a dark, fern-fringed cave. He strips away lightly, delicately, gently, all the trappings of our feverish worldliness, our vanity and ambition, and lifts open, at one touch, the great moon-bathed windows that look out upon the line of white foam—and the patient sands.

And never is this calm deeper than when he refers to Death. "For there," he says, speaking of that Cemetery at Firenze where his Thyrsis lies;
"For there thine earth-forgetting eyelids keep
"The morningless and unawakening sleep,
"Under the flowery Oleanders pale—"
Sometimes, as in his "Tristram and Iseult," he is permitted little touches of a startling and

penetrating beauty; such as, returning to one's memory and lips, in very dusty and arid places, bring all the tears of half-forgotten romance back again to us and restore to us the despair that is dearer than hope!

Those lines, for instance, when Tristram, dying in his fire-lit, tapestried room, tended by the pale Iseult of Brittany, knows that his death-longing is fulfilled, and that she, his "other" Iseult, has come to him at last—have they not the very echo in them of what such weariness feels when, only not too late, the impossible happens? Little he cares for the rain beating on the roof, or the moan of the wind in the chimney, or the shadows on that tapestried wall! He listens—his heart almost stops.

"What voices are those in the still night air? What lights in the court? What steps on the
   stair?"

One wonders if the reader, too, knows and loves, that strange fragmentary unrhymed poem, called "the Strayed Reveller," with its vision of Circe and the sleeping boy-faun, and the wave-tossed Wanderer, and its background of "fitful earth-murmurs" and "dreaming woods"—Strangely down, upon the weary child, smiles the great enchantress, seeing the wine stains on his white skin, and the berries in his hair. The thing is slight enough; but in its coolness, and calmness, and sad delicate

MATTHEW ARNOLD

beauty, it makes one pause and grow silent, as in the long hushed galleries of the Vatican one pauses and grows silent before some little known, scarcely-catalogued Greek Vase. The spirit of life and youth is there—immortal and tender—yet there too is the shadow of that pitiful "in vain," with which the brevity of such beauty, arrested only in chilly marble, mocks us as we pass!

It is life—but life at a distance—Life refined, winnowed, sifted, purged. "Yet, O Prince, what labour! O Prince, what pain!" The world is perhaps tired of hearing from the mouths of its great lonely exiles the warning to youth "to sink unto its own soul," and let the mad throngs clamour by, with their beckoning idols, and treacherous pleading. But never has this unregarded hand been laid so gently upon us as in the poem called "Self-Dependence."

Heaven forgive us—we cannot follow its high teaching—and yet we too, we all, have felt that sort of thing, when standing at the prow of a great ship we have watched the reflection of the stars in the fast-divided water.
"Unaffrightened by the silence round them
"Undistracted by the sights they see
"These demand not that the world about them
"Yield them love, amusement, sympathy.
"But with joy the stars perform their shining
"And the sea its long, moon-silvered roll;

"For self-poised they live; nor pine with noting
"All the fever of some differing soul."
The "one philosophy" is, as Matthew Arnold himself puts it, "utrumque paratus," prepared for either event. Yet it leans, and how should it not lean, in a world like this, to the sadder and the more final. That vision of a godless universe, "rocking its obscure body to and fro," in ghastly space, is a vision that refuses to pass away. "To the children of chance," as my Catholic philosopher says, "chance would seem intelligible."

But even if it be—if the whole confluent ocean of its experiences be—unintelligible and without meaning; it remains that mortal men must endure it, and comfort themselves with their "little pleasures." The immoral cruelty of Fate has been well expressed by Matthew Arnold in that poem called "Mycerinus," where the virtuous king *does not* receive his reward. He, for his part will revel and care not. There may be nobler, there may be happier, ways of awaiting the end—but whether "revelling" or "refraining," we are all waiting the end. Waiting and listening, half-bitterly, half-eagerly, seems the lot of man upon earth! And meanwhile that

———— "Power, too great and strong
"Even for the gods to conquer or beguile,
"Sweeps earth and heaven and men and gods along

MATTHEW ARNOLD

"Like the broad volume of the insurgent Nile
"And the great powers we serve, themselves must be
"Slaves of a tyrannous Necessity———"

Matthew Arnold had—and it is a rare gift—in spite of his peaceful domestic life and in spite of that "interlude" of the "Marguerite" poems—a noble and a chaste soul. "Give me a clean heart, O God, and renew a right spirit within me!" prayed the Psalmist. Well! this friend of Thyrsis had "a clean heart" and "a right spirit"; and these things, in this turbulent age, have their appeal! It was the purging of this "hyssop" that made it possible for him even in the "Marguerite" poems, to write as only those can write whose passion is more than the craving of the flesh.

"Come to me in my dreams and then
"In sleep I shall be well again—
"For then the night will more than pay
"The hopeless longing of the day!"

It was the same chastity of the senses that made it possible for him to write those verses upon a young girl's death, which are so much more beautiful—though *those* are lovely too—than the ones Oscar Wilde wrote on the same subject.

"Strew on her, roses, roses,
"But never a spray of yew;
"For in silence she reposes—

"Ah! would that I did too!
"Her cabined ample spirit
"It fluttered and failed for breath.
"Tonight it doth inherit
"The vasty halls of death.

Matthew Arnold is one of the poets who have what might be called "the power of Liberation." He liberates us from the hot fevers of our lusts. He liberates us from our worldliness, our perversions, our mad preoccupations. He reduces things to their simple elements and gives us back air and water and land and sea. And he does this without demanding from us any unusual strain. We have no need to plunge into Dionysian ecstacies, or cry aloud after "cosmic emotion."

We have no need to relinquish our common sense; or to dress or eat or talk or dream, in any strange manner. It is enough if we remember the fields where we were born. It is enough if we do not altogether forget out of what quarter of the sky Orion rises; and where the lord-star Jupiter has his place. It is enough if we are not quite oblivious of the return of the Spring and the sprouting of the first leaves.

From the poetry of Matthew Arnold it is possible to derive an art of life which carries us back to the beginnings of the world's history. He, the civilized Oxonian; he, domestic moralist; he, the airily playful scholar, has yet the power of giving that *Epic solemnity* to our sleep and our waking; to our "going forth to our work and our labour until the evening"; to the passing of the seasons over us; which is the ground and substance of all poetic imagination, and which no change or progress, or discovery, can invade or spoil.

For it is the nature of poetry to heighten and to throw into relief those eternal things in our common destiny which too soon get overlaid—And some things only poetry can reach—Religion may have small comfort for us when in the secret depths of our hearts we endure a craving of which we may not speak, a sickening aching longing for "the lips so sweetly forsworn." But poetry is waiting for us, there also, with her Rosemary and her Rue. Not one human heart but has its hidden shrine before which the professional ministrants are fain to hold their peace. But even there, under the veiled Figure itself, some poor poetic "Jongleur de Notre Dame" is permitted to drop his monk's robe, and dance the dance that makes time and space nothing!

SHELLEY

SHELLEY

NE of the reasons why we find it hard to read the great poets is that they sadden us with their troubling beauty. Sadden us—and put us to shame! They compel us to remember the days of our youth; and that is more than most of us are able to bear! What memories! Ye gods, what memories!

And this is true, above all, of Shelley. His verses, when we return to them again, seem to have the very "perfume and suppliance" of the Spring; of the Spring of our frost-bitten age. Their sweetness has a poignancy and a pang; the sweetness of things too dear; of things whose beauty brings aching and a sense of bitter loss. It is the sudden uncovering of dead violets, with the memory of the soil they were plucked from. It is the strain of music over wide waters—and over wider years.

These verses always had something about them that went further than their actual meaning. They were always a little like planetary melodies, to which earthly words had been fitted. And now they carry us, not only beyond words, but beyond thought,—"as doth Eternity." There is, indeed, a sadness such as one cannot bear long "and live" about Shelley's poetry.

It troubles our peace. It passes over the sterility of our poor comfort like a lost child's cry. It beats upon the door. It rattles the shut casement. It sobs with the rain upon the roof. This is partly because Shelley, more than any poet, has entered into the loneliness of the elements, and given up his heart to the wind, and his soul to the outer darkness. The other poets can *describe* these things, but he *becomes* what they are. Listening to him, we listen to them. And who can bear to listen to them? Who, in cold blood, can receive the sorrows of the "many waters"? Who can endure while the heavens, that are "themselves so old," bend down with the burden of their secret?

Not to "describe," but to share the life, or the death-in-life, of the thing you write of, that is the true poetic way. The "arrowy odours" of those first white violets he makes us feel, darting forth from among the dead leaves, do they leave us content with the art of their description? They provoke us with their fine essence. They trouble us with a fatality we have to share. The passing from its "caverns of rain" of the newborn cloud—we do not only follow it, obedient to the spell of rhetoric; we are whirled forward with it, laughing at its "cenotaph" and our own, into unimagined ærial spaces. One feels all this and more under Shelley's influence—but alas! as soon as one has felt it, the old cynical, realistic mood descends again, "heavy as frost," and the vision of ourselves, poor, straggling, forked animals, caught up into such regions, shows but as a pantomimic farce; and we awake, shamed and clothed, and in our "right mind!"

With some poets, with Milton and Matthew Arnold, for example, there is always a kind of implicit sub-reference, accompanying the heroic gesture or the magical touch, to our poor normal humanity. With others, with Tennyson or Browning, for instance, one is often rather absurdly aware of the worthy Victorian Person, behind the poetic mask, "singing" his ethical ditty—like a great, self-conscious speckled thrush upon a prominent bough.

But with Shelley everything is forgotten. It is the authentic fury, the divine madness; and we pass out of ourselves, and "suffer a sea-change into something rich and strange." Into something "strange," perhaps, rather than something "rich"; for the temperament of Shelley, like that of Corot, leads him to suppress the more glowing threads of Nature's woof; leads him to dissolve everything in filmy white light; in the light of an impossible dawn. Has it been noticed how all material objects dissolve at his touch, and float away, as mists and vapours? He has, it seems, an almost insane predilection for *white* things. White violets, white pansies, white windflowers, white ghosts, white daisies and white moons thrill us, as we read, with an almost unearthly awe. White Death, too; the shadow of white Corruption, has her place there, and the appalling whiteness of lepers and corpses. The liturgy he chants is the liturgy of the White Mass, and the "white radiance" of Eternity is his Real Presence.

Weird and fantastic though Shelley's dreams may appear, it is more than likely that some of them will be realized before we expect it. His passionate advocacy of what now is called "Feminism," his sublime revolutionary hopes for the proletariat, his denunciation of war, his arraignment of so-called "Law" and "Order," his indictment of conventional Morality, his onslaughts on outworn Institutions, his invectives against Hypocrisy and Stupidity, are not by any means the blind Utopian rhetoric that some have called them. That crafty slur upon brave new thought which we know so well—that "how-can-you-take-him-seriously" attitude of the "status-quo" rascals —must not mislead us with regard to Shelley's philosophy.

He is a genuine philosopher, as well as a dreamer. Or shall we say he is the only kind of philosopher who *must* be taken seriously—

SHELLEY

the philosopher who creates the dreams of the young?

Shelley is, indeed, a most rare and invaluable thinker, as well as a most exquisite poet. His thought and his poetry can no more be separated than could the thought and poetry of the Book of Job. His poetry is the embodiment of his thought, its swift and splendid incarnation.

Strange though it may seem, there are not very many poets who have the particular kind of *ice-cold intellect* necessary if one is to detach one's self completely from the idols of the market-place. Indeed, the poetic temperament is only too apt, out of the very warmth of its sensitive humanity, to idealize the old traditions and throw a glamour around them. That is why, both in politics and religion, there have been, ever since Aristophanes, so many great reactionary poets. Their warmth of human sympathy, their "nihil alienum" attitude; nay! their very sense of humour, have made this inevitable. There is so often, too, something chilly and "unhomely," something pitiless and cruel, about quite rational reform, which alienates the poetic mind. It must be remembered that the very thing that makes so many objects poetical—I mean their *traditional association* with normal human life—is the thing that *has to be destroyed* if the new birth is to take place. The ice-cold austerity of mind, indicated in the superb contempt of the Nietzschean phrase, "human, too human," is a mood essential, if the world is to cast off its "weeds outworn." Change and growth, when they are living and organic, imply the element of destruction. It is easy enough to talk smoothly about natural "evolution." What Nature herself does, as we are beginning to realize at last, is to advance by leaps and bounds. One of these mad leaps having produced the human brain, it is *for us* to follow her example and slough off another Past. Man is *that which has to be left behind!* We thus begin to see what I must be allowed to call the essential inhumanity of the true prophet. The false prophet is known by nothing so easily as by his crying "peace"—his crying, "hands off! enough!"

It is tragic to think how little the world has changed since Shelley's time, and how horribly relevant to the present hour are his outcries against Militarism, Capitalism and Privilege. If evidence were wanted of the profound moral value of Shelley's revolutionary thought, one has only to read the proclamations of any international school of Socialistic propaganda, and find how they are fighting now what he fought then. His ideas have never been more necessary than they are today. Tolstoi has preached some of them, Bernard Shaw others, and Mr. Wells yet others. But none of our modern rebels have managed to give to their new thought quite the comprehensiveness and daring which we find in him.

And he has achieved this by the intensity of his devotion. Modern literary Anarchists are so inclined to fall into jocularity, and irony, and "human, too human" humour. Their Hamlet-like consciousness of the "many mansions" of truth tends to paralyse the impetus of their challenge. They are so often, too, dramatists and novelists rather than prophets, and their work, while it gains in sympathy and subtlety, loses in directness. The immense encouragement given to really drastic, original thought by Nietzsche's writings is an evidence of the importance of what might be called *cruel positivity* in human thinking. Shelley has, however, an advantage over Nietzsche in his recognition of the transformative power of "love." In this respect, iconoclast though he is, he is rather with the Buddha and the Christ than with the modern antinomians.

His *mania* for "love"—one can call it nothing else—frees his revolutionary thought from that arbitrary isolation, that savage subjectivity, which one notes in many philosophical anarchists. His Platonic insistence, too, on the more spiritual aspects of "love" separates his anti-Christian "Immorality" from the easy-going, pleasant hedonism of such a bold individualist as Remy de Gourmont.

Shelley's individualism is always a thing with open doors; a thing with corridors into Eternity. It never conveys that sad, cynical, pessimistic sense of "eating and drinking" before we die, which one is so familiar with just now.

It is precisely this fact that those who reprobate Shelley's "immorality" should remember. With him "love" was truly a mystical initiation, a religious sacrament, a means of getting into touch with the cosmic secret, a path—and perhaps the only path—to the Beatific Vision.

It is not wise to turn away from Shelley because of his lack of "humour," of his lack of a "sense of proportion." The mystery of the world, whatever it may be, shows itself sometimes quite as indifferent as Shelley to these little nuances. We hear it crying aloud in the night with no humorous cry; and it is too often to stop our ears to what we hear, that we jest so lightly! It is doubtful whether Nature cares greatly for our "sense of proportion."

To return to his poetry, as poetry. The remarkable thing about Shelley's verse is the manner in which his whole physical and psychic temperament has passed into it. This is so in a measure with all poets, but it is so especially with him. His beautiful epicene face, his boyish figure, his unearthly sensitiveness,

SHELLEY

haunt us as we read his lines. They allure and baffle us, as the smile on the lips of the Mona Lisa. One has the impression of listening to a being who has really traversed the ways of the sea and returned with its secret. How else could those indescribable pearly shimmerings, those opal tints and rosy shadows, be communicated to our poor language? The very purity of his nature, that ethereal quality in it that strikes a chill into the heart of "normal humanity," lends a magic, like the reflection of moonlight upon ice, to these inter-lunar melodies. The same ethereal transparency of passion which excites, by reason of its sublime "immorality," the gross fury of the cynical and the base, gives an immortal beauty, cold and distant and beyond "the shadow of our night," to his planetary melodies. It is, indeed, the old Pythagorean "music of the spheres" audible at last again. Such sounds has the *silence* that descends upon us when we look up, above the roofs of the city, at Arcturus or Aldeboran! To return to Shelley from the turmoil of our gross excitements and cramped domesticities is to bathe our foreheads in the "dew of the morning" and cool our hands in the ultimate Sea. Whatever in us transcends the vicious circle of personal desire; whatever in us belongs to that Life which lasts while we and our individual cravings perish; whatever in us underlies and overlooks this mad procession of "births and forgettings;" whatever in us "beacons from the abode where the Eternal are," rises to meet this celestial harmony, and sloughs off the "muddy vesture" that would "grossly close it in." What separates Shelley from all other poets is that with them "art" is the paramount concern, and, after "art," morality.

With him one thinks little of art, little of the substance of any material "teaching;" one is simply transported into the high, cold regions where the creative gods build, like children, domes of "many-coloured glass," wherewith to "stain the white radiance of eternity." And after such a plunge into the antenatal reservoirs of life, we may, if we can, go on spitting venom and raking in the gutter with the old too-human zest, and let the "ineffectual" madman pass and be forgotten!

I said that the effect of his writing is to trouble and sadden us. It was as a man I spoke. That in us which responds to Shelley's verse is precisely what dreams of the transmutation of "man" into "beyond-man." That which saddens humanity beyond words is the daily food of the immortals.

And yet, even in the circle of our natural moods, there is something, sometimes, that responds to such strains as "When the lamp is shattered" and "One word is too often profaned." Perhaps only those who have known

SHELLEY

what it is to love as children love, and to lose hope with the absoluteness wherewith children lose it, can enter competely into this delicate despair. It is, indeed, the long, pitiful, sobbing cry of bewildered disenchantment that breaks the heart of youth when it first learns of what gross clay earth and men are made.

And the artless simplicity of Shelley's technique—much more really simple than the conscious "childishness," exquisite though that is, of a Blake or Verlaine—lends itself so wonderfully to the expression of youth's eternal sorrow. His best lyrics use words that fall into their places with the "dying fall" of an actual fit of sobbing. And they are so naturally chosen, his images and metaphors! Even when they seem most remote, they are such as frail young hearts cannot help happening upon, as they soothe their "love-laden souls" in "secret hour."

The infallible test of genuine poetry is that it forces us to recall emotions that we ourselves have had, with the very form and circumstance of their passion. And who can read the verses of Shelley without recalling such? That peculiar poignancy of memory, like a sharp spear, which arrests us at the smell of certain plants or mosses, or nameless earth-mould, or "growths by the margins of pond-waters;" that poignancy which brings back the indescribable balm of Spring and the bitter-sweetness of irremediable loss; who can communicate it like Shelley?

There are lovely touches of foreign scenery in his poems, particularly of the vineyards and olive gardens and clear-cut hill towns of Italy; but for English readers it will always be the rosemary "that is for remembrance" and the pansies that "are for thoughts" that give their perfume to the feelings he excites.

Other poets may be remembered at other times, but it is when the sun-warmed woods smell of the first primroses, and the daffodils, coming "before the swallow dares," lift up their heads above the grass, that the sting of this sweetness, too exquisite to last beyond a moment, brings its intolerable hope and its intolerable regret.

KEATS

KEATS

T is well that there should be at least one poet of Beauty—of Beauty alone —of Beauty and naught else. It is well that one should dare to follow that terrible goddess even to the bitter end. That pitiless marble altar has its victims, as the other Altars. The "white implacable Aphrodite" cries aloud for blood—for the blood of our dearest affections; for the blood of our most cherished hopes; for the blood of our integrity and faith; for the blood of our reason. She drugs us, blinds us, tortures us, maddens us, and slays us—yet we follow her—to the bitter end!

Beauty hath her Martyrs, as the rest; and of these Keats is the Protagonist; the youngest and the fairest; the most enamoured victim. From those extraordinary letters of his, to his friends and to his love, we gather that this fierce amorist of Beauty was not without his Philosophy. The Philosophy of Keats, as we gather up the threads of it, one by one, in those fleeting confessions, is nothing but the old polytheistic paganism, reduced to terms of modern life. He was a born "Pluralist," to use the modern phrase; and for him, in this congeries of separate and unique miracles, which we call the World, there was neither Unity, nor Progress, nor Purpose, nor Over-soul—nothing but the mystery of Beauty, and the Memory of great men!

His way of approaching Nature, his way of approaching every event in life, was "pluralistic." He did not ask that things should come in upon him in logical order or in rational coherence. He only asked that each unique person who appeared; each unique hill-side or meadow or hedgerow or vineyard or flower or tree; should be for him a new incarnation of Beauty, a new avatar of the merciless One he followed.

Never has there been a poet less *mystical*—never a poet less *moral*. The ground and soil, and sub-soil, of his nature, was Sensuality—a rich, quivering, tormented Sensuality!

If you will, you may use, for what he was, the word "materialistic"; but such a word gives an absurdly wrong impression. The physical nerves of his abnormally troubled senses, were too exquisitely, too passionately stirred, to let their vibrations die away in material bondage. They quiver off into remotest psychic waves, these shaken strings; and a touch will send them shuddering into the high regions of the Spirit. For a nature like this, with the fever of consumption wasting his tissues, and the fever of his thirst for Beauty ravaging his soul, it was nothing less than the cruellest tragedy that he should have been driven by the phantom-flame of sex-illusion to find all the magic and wonder of the Mystery he worshiped, caught, imprisoned, enclosed, *blighted,* in the poisonous loveliness of one capricious girl. An anarchist at heart—as so many great artists are—Keats hated, with a furious hatred, any bastard claims and privileges that insolently intruded themselves between the godlike senses of Man and the divine madness of their quest. Society? the Public? Moral Opinion? Intellectual Fashion? The manners and customs of the Upper Classes? What were all these but vain impertinences, interrupting his desperate Pursuit? "Every gentleman" he cried "is my natural enemy!"

The feverish fanaticism of his devotion knew absolutely no limits. His cry day and night was for "new sensations"; and such "sensation," a mere epicurean indulgence to others, was a lust, a madness, a frenzy, a fury, a rushing upon death, to him.

How young he was, how pitifully young, when the Foam-born, jealous of him as she was jealous of Hyppolytus, hurled him bleeding to the ground!

But what Poetry he has left behind him! There is nothing like it in the world. Nothing like it, for sheer, deadly, draining, maddening, drowsing witchery of beauty. It is the very cup of Circe—the very philtre of Sun-poison. "A thing of Beauty is a Joy forever"! A Joy? Yes—but a Joy *drugged* from its first pouring forth. We follow. We have to follow. But, O the weariness of the way!

What an exultant hymn that is,—the one in honour of Pan, which comes so soon in Endymion! The dim rich depths of the dark forests are stirred by it, and its murmurs die away, over the wailing spaces of the marshes. Obscure growths, and drowsy weeds overhanging moon-lit paths, where fungoid things fumble for light and air, hear that cry in their voluptuous dreams and move uneasily. The dumb vegetable *expectancy* of young tree-trunks is roused by it into sensual terror. For this is the sound of the hoof of Pan, stamping on the moist earth, as he rages for Syrinx. No one has ever understood the torment of the Wood-god and his mad joy, as the author of Endymion understood them. The tumultuous ground-swell of this poet's insane craving for Beauty must in the end have driven him on the rocks; but there came sometimes softer, gentler, less "vermeil-tinctured" moods, which might have prolonged his days, had he never met "that girl."

"The Pot of Basil" expresses one of these. Wistful and heart-breaking, it has a tender yearning *pity* in it, a gentle melancholy brooding, over the irremediable pain of love-loss, which haunts one like the sound of drowned Angelus-bells, under a hushed sea. The description of the appearance of the ghost of the dead boy and his vague troubled speech, is like nothing else that has ever been written.

St. Agnes Eve too, in its more elaborate, more premeditated art, has a beauty so poignant, so *sensuously unearthly,* that one dare not quote a line of it, in a mere "critical essay," for fear of breaking such a spell!

The long-drawn solemn harmonies of "Hyperion"—Miltonian, and yet troubled by a thrilling sorcery that Milton never knew—madden the reader with anger that he never finished it; an anger which is only increased when in that other "Version," the influence of Dante becomes evident. "La Belle Dame Sans Merci!" Ah, there we find him—there we await him—the poet of *the tragedy of bodily craving,* transferred, with all its aching, famished nerves, on to the psychic plane!

For "La Belle Dame" is the Litany of the Beauty-Maniac—his death-in-life Requiem, his eternal Dirge! Those who have ever met Her, this "Lady in the mead, full-beautiful, a fairy-child," whose foot "was light" and whose hair "was long" and whose eyes "were wild," will know—and only they—the meaning of "the starved lips, through the gloom, with horrid warning, gaping wide"! And has the secret of the gasping pause of that broken half-line, "where no birds sing," borrowed originally from poor Ophelia's despair, and echoed wonderfully by Mr. Hardy in certain of his incomparable lyrics, been conveyed to my reader?

But it is, of course, in his five great Odes, that Keats is most supreme, most entirely, without question, the unapproachable artist. Heaven forbid that I should shatter the sacred silence that such things produce, by any profane repetition! They leave behind them, every one of them, an echo, a vibration, a dying fall, leaving us enchanted and trembling; as when we have been touched, before the twittering of the birds at dawn, by the very fingers of Our Lady of sweet Pain!

Is it possible that words, mere words, can work such miracles? Or are they not words at all, but chalices and Holy graals, of human passion, full of the life-blood, staining the lips that approach them scarlet, of heart-drained pulse-wearied ravishment?

Certainly he has the touch, ineffable, final, absolute, of the supreme Beauty. And over it all, over the ardours and ecstasies, hangs the shadow of Death; and in the heart of it, an adder in the deep drugged cup, coiled and waiting, the poisonous bite of incurable anguish! We may stand mesmerized, spell-bound, amid

KEATS

"the hushed cool-rooted flowers, fragrant-eyed" watching Psyche sleep. We may open those "charmed magic casements" towards "the perilous foam." We may linger with Ruth "sick for home amid the alien corn." We may gaze, awed and hushed, at the dead, cold, little, mountain-built town, "emptied of its folks"—We may "glut our sorrow on the morning rose, or on the wealth of globéd Peonies." We may "imprison our mistress's soft hand, and gaze, deep, deep, within her peerless eyes." We may brood, quieted and sweetly-sad, upon the last melancholy "oozings" of the rich year's vintage. But across all these things lies, like a streak of red, breath-catching, spilled heart's blood, the knowledge of *what it means* to have been able to turn all this into poetry!

It means Torment. It means Despair. It means *that cry,* out of the dust of the cemetery at Rome, "O God! O God! has there ever been such pain as my pain?"

I suppose Keats suffered more in his brief life than any mortal child of the Muses. These ultimate creations of supreme Beauty are evoked in no other way. Everything has to be sacrificed—everything—if we are to be—like the gods, *creators of Life.* For Life is a thing that can only be born in *that soil*—only planted where the wound goes deepest—only watered when we strike where that fountain flows!

He wrote for himself. The crowd, the verdict of his friends—what did all that matter? He wrote for himself; and for those who dare to risk the taste of that wine, which turns the taste of all else to a weary irrelevance!

One is unwilling to leave our Adonais, whose "annual wound in Lebanon allures" us thus fatally, with nothing but such a bitter cry. One has a pathetic human longing to think of him *as he was,* in those few moments of unalloyed pleasure the gods allowed him before "consumption," and "that girl," poisoned the springs of his life! And those moments, how they have passed into his poetry like the breath of the Spring!

When "the grand obsession" was not upon him, who, like Keats, can make us feel the cool, sweet, wholesome touch of our great Mother, the Earth? That sleep, "full of sweet dreams and health and quiet breathing," which the breast that suckled Persephone alone can give may heal us also for a brief while.

We, too, on this very morning—listen reader!—may wreath " a flowery band to bind us to the Earth, spite of despondence." Some "shape of beauty may yet move away the pall from our dark spirits." Even with old Saturn under his weight of grief, we may drink in the loveliness of those "green-robed senators of mighty woods, tall oaks, branch-charmèd by the earnest stars." And in the worst of our

moods we can still call aloud to the things of beauty that pass not away. We can even call out to them from her very side who is "the cause," "the cause, my soul," of what we suffer. "Bright star, would I were steadfast as thou art!
  Not in lone splendour hung aloft the night,
  And watching, with eternal lids apart,
  Like Nature's patient, sleepless eremite,
  The moving waters at their priest-like task
  Of pure ablution round earth's human shores—"
This desperate, sensuous pain which makes us cry out to the "midnight" that we might "cease upon it," need not harden our hearts before we pass hence. The "gathering swallows twittering in the sky" of our little interludes of peace may still attune us to some strange, sad thankfulness that we have been born into life, even though life turned out to mean *this!*

And the vibrating, stricken nerves of our too great devotion may have at least the balm of feeling that they have not languished untouched by the fingers that thrill while they slay. After all, "we have lived"; we also; and we would not "change places" with those "happy innocents" who have never known the madness of what it may be to have been born a son of man!

But let none be deluded. The tragic life upon earth is not the life of the spirit, but the life of the senses. The senses are the aching doors to the greatest mystery of all, the mystery of our tyranny over one another. Does anyone think that that love is greater, more real, more poignant, which can stand over the dead body of its One-of-all, and dream of encounters and reconciliations, in other worlds? It is not so! What we have loved is cold, cold and dead, and has become *that thing* we scarcely recognise. Can any vague, spiritual reunion make up for the loss of the little gestures, the little touches, *the little ways,* we shall never through all eternity know again? Ah! those reluctances and hesitations, over now, quite over now! Ah! those fretful pleadings, those strange withdrawals, those unheeded protests; nothing, less than nothing, and mere memories! When the life of the senses invades the affections of the heart—then, then, mon enfant, comes the pinch and the sting!

And this is what happens with such doomed sensualists as Keats was. What tortured him in death was the thought that he must leave his darling—and the actual look, touch, air, ways and presence of her, forever. "Vain," as that inspired Lover, Emily Bronte, cries, "vain, unutterably vain, are 'all the creeds' that would console!" Tired of hearing "simple truth miscalled simplicity"; tired of all the weariness of life—from these we "would begone"—"save that to die we leave our love alone"!

KEATS

But it is not only in the fatal danger of eternal separation from the flesh that has become to us moré necessary than sun or moon, that *the tragedy of the senses lies.* It lies in the very intensity with which we have sifted, winnowed, tormented and refined these panthers of holy lust. Those who understand the poetry of Keats recognise that in the passion which burns him for the "heavenly quintessence," as Marlowe calls it, there is also the ghastly danger of reaction. The pitiless hands of Joy "are ever at his lips, bidding adieu," and "veiled melancholy has her 'sovran shrine' in the heart of all delight."

This is the curse upon those who follow the *supreme Beauty*—that is to say, the Beauty that belongs, not to ideas and ideals, but to living forms. They are driven by the gross pressure of circumstance to forsake her, to leave her, to turn aside and eat husks with the swine!

It is the same with that supreme mystery of *words* themselves, out of which such an artist as this one was creates his spells and his sorcery. How, after tasting, drop by drop, that draught of "lingered sweetness long drawn-out" of his unequalled style, can we bear to fall back upon the jabbering and screeching, the howling and hissing, of the voices we have to listen to in common resort? Ah, child, child! Think carefully before you turn your candid-innocent eyes to the fatal entrance to these mysteries!. It is better never to have known what the high, terrible loveliness of Her of Melos is than, *having seen her,* to pass the rest of our days with these copies, and prostitutions, and profanations, and parodies, "which mimic humanity so abominably"!

That is the worst of it. That is the sting of it. All the *great quests* in this world tempt us and destroy us, for, though they may touch our famished lips once and again before we perish, one thing they cannot do—one thing Beauty herself, the most sacred of all such quests, cannot do—and that is to make the arid intervals of our ordinary life tolerable, when we have to return to the common world, and the people and things that stand gaping in that world, like stupid, staring idols!

But what matter? Let us pay the penalty. Let us pay the price. *Is it not worth it?* Beauty! O divine, O cruel Mistress! Thee, thee we must worship still, and with thee the acolytes who bear thy censers! For the secret of life is to take every risk without fear; even the risk of finding one's self an exile, with "no shrine, no grove, no oracle, no heat of palemouthed prophet dreaming" in the land without memories, without altars, without Thee!

NIETZSCHE

NIETZSCHE

T is not the hour in which to say much about Nietzsche. The dissentient voices are silent. The crowd has stopped howling. But a worse thing is happening to him, the thing of all others he dreaded most;—he is becoming "accepted"—The preachers are quoting him and the theologians are explaining him.

What he would himself pray for now are Enemies—fierce irreconcilable Enemies—but our age cannot produce such. It can only produce sneering disparagement; or frightened conventional approbation.

What one would like to say, at this particular juncture, is that *here,* or again *there,* this deadly antagonist of God missed his aim. But who can say that? He aimed too surely. No, he did not miss his aim. He smote whom he went out to smite. But one thing he could not smite; he could neither smite it, or unmask it, or "transvalue" it. I mean the Earth itself—the great, shrewd, wise, all-enduring Mother of us all—who knows so much, and remains so silent!

VISIONS AND REVISIONS

And sometimes one feels, walking some country road, with the smell of upturned sods and heavy leaf-mould in one's nostrils, that even Lucifer himself is not as deep or strong or wise as is patient furrowed earth and her blundering children. A rough earth-hint, a Rabelaisian ditty, a gross amazing jest, a chuckle of deep Satyric humour;—and the monstrous "thickness" of Life, its friendly aplomb and nonchalence, its grotesque irreverence, its shy shrewd common-sense, its tough fibres, and portentous indifference to "distinction"; tumbles us over in the mud—for all our "aloofness"—and roars over us, like a romping bull-calf!

The antidote to Nietzsche is not to be found in the company of the Saints. He was too much of a Saint himself for that. It is to be found in the company of Shakespearean clodhoppers, and Rabelaisian topers, and Cervantian serving-wenches. In fact, it is to be found, as with the antidotes for other noble excesses, in burying your face in rough moist earth; and grubbing for pig-nuts under the beech-trees. A summer's day in the woods with Audrey will put "Fatality" into its place and remove "the Recurrence of all things" to a very modest remoteness. And this is not a relinquishing of the secret of life. This is not a giving up of the supreme quest. It is an opening of another door; a letting in of a different air; a reversion to a more primitive level of the mystery.

The way to reduce the tyranny of this proud spirit to its proper proportion is not to talk about "Love" or "Morality" or "Orthodoxy," or "the strength of the vulgar herd"—it is simply to call up in one's mind the motley procession of gross, simple, quaint, *bulbous,* irrepressible objects—human and otherwise—whose mere existence makes it as impossible for Nietzsche to deal with the *massiveness* of Life, as it is impossible for anyone else to deal with it.

No, we shall not free ourselves from his intellectual predominence by taking refuge with the Saints. We shall not do this because he himself was essentially a Saint. A Saint and a Martyr! Is it for me now to prove that?

It is realized, I suppose, what the history of his spiritual contest actually was? It was a deliberate self-inflicted Crucifixion of the Christ in him, as an offering to the Apollo in him. Nietzsche was—that cannot be denied—an Intellectual Sadist; and his Intellectual Sadism took the form—as it can (he has himself taught us so) take many curious forms—of deilberately outraging his own most sensitive nerves. This is really what broke his reason, in the end. By a process of spiritual vivisection—the suffering of which one dare not conceive—he took his natural "sanctity," and carved it, as a dish fit for the gods, until it assumed an Apollonian shape. We must visualize Nietzsche not only as the Philosopher with the Hammer; but as the Philosopher with the Chisel.

We must visualize him, with such a sculptor's tool, standing in the presence of the crucified figure of himself; and altering one by one, its natural lineaments! Nietzsche's own lacerated "intellectual nerves" were the vantage-ground of his spiritual vision. He could write "the Antichrist," because he had "killed," in his own nature, "the thing he loved." It was for this reason that he had such a supernatural insight into the Christian temperament. It was for this reason that he could pour vitrol upon its "little secrets"; and hunt it to its last retreats.

Let none think he did not understand the grandeur, and the terrible intoxicating appeal, of the thing he fought. He understood these only too well. What vibrating sympathy—as for a kindred spirit—may be read between the lines of his attack on Pascal—Pascal, the supreme type of the Christian Philosopher!

It must be further realized—for after all what are words and phrases?—that it was really nothing but the "Christian conscience" in him that forced him on so desperately to kick against the pricks. It was the "Christian conscience" in him—has he not himself analysed the voluptuous cruelty of that?—which drove him to seek something—if possible—nobler, austerer, gayer, more innocently wicked, than Christianity!

It was not in the interests of Truth that he fought it. True Christian, as he was, at heart, he never cared greatly for Truth as Truth. It was in the interest of a Higher Ideal, a more exacting, less human Ideal, that he crushed it down. The Christian spirit, in him set him upon strangling the Christian spirit—and all in the interest of a madness of nobility, itself perforated with Christian conscience!

Was Nietzsche really Greek, compared with —Goethe, let us say? Not for a moment. It was in the desperation of his attempt to be so, that he seized upon Greek tragedy and made it dance to Christian cymbals! This is, let it be clearly understood, the hidden secret of his mania for Dionysus—Dionysus gave him his opportunity. In the worship of this god—also a wounded god, be it remarked;—he was able to satisfy his perverted craving for "ecstasy of laceration" under the shadow of another Name.

But after all—as Goethe says—"feeling is all in all; the name is sound and smoke." What he felt were Christian feelings, the feelings of a Mystic, a Visionary, a Flagellant. What matter by what name you call them? Christ? Dionysus? It is the secret creative passion of the human heart that sends them Both forth upon their warfaring.

Is any one simple enough to think that whatever Secret Cosmic Power melts into human ecstasy, it waits to be summoned by certain particular syllables? That this arbitrary strangling of the Christ in him never altogether ended, is proved by the words of those tragic messages he sent to Cosima Wagner from "the aristocratic city of Turin" when his tormented brain broke like a taut bow-string. Those messages resembled arrows of fire, shot into space; and on one was written the words "The Crucified" and on the other the word "Dionysus."

The grand and heart-breaking appeal of this lonely Victim of his own merciless scourge, does not depend, for its effect upon us, upon any of the particular "ideas" he announced. The idea of the "Eternal Recurrence of all things"—to take the most terrible—is clearly but another instance of his intellectual Sadism.

The worst thing that could happen to those innumerable Victims of Life, for whom he sought to kill his Pity, was that they should have to go through the same punishment again —not once or twice, but for an infinity of times—and it was just that that he, whose immense Pity for them took so long a killing, suddenly felt must be what *had* to happen—had to happen for no other reason than that it was

NIETZSCHE

intolerable that it should happen. Again, we may note, it was not "Truth" he sought, but ecstasy, and, in this case, the ecstasy of "accepting" the very worst kind of issue he could possibly imagine.

The idea of the Superman, too, is an idea that could only have entered the brain of one, pushed on to think, at the spear-head of his own cruelty. It is a great and terrible idea, sublime and devastating, this idea of the human race yielding place to *another race,* stronger, wiser, fairer, sterner, gayer, and more godlike! Especially noble and compelling is Nietzsche's constant insistence that the moment has come for men to take their Destiny out of the blind power of Evolution, and to guide it themselves, with a strong hand and a clear will, towards a *definite goal.*

The fact that this driving force, of cruelty to himself and, through himself, to humanity, scourged him on to so formidable an illumination of our path, is a proof how unwise it is to suppress any grand perversion. Such motive-forces should be used, as Nietzsche used his, for purposes of intellectual insight—not simply trampled upon as "evil."

Whether our poor human race ever will surpass itself, as he demands, and rise to something psychologically different, "may admit a wide solution." It is not an unscientific idea. It is not an irreligious idea. It has all the dreams of the Prophets behind it. But—who can tell? It is quite as possible that the spirit of destruction in us will wantonly ruin this great Chance as that we shall seize upon it. Man has many other impulses besides the impulse of creation. Perhaps he will never be seduced into even *desiring* such a goal, far less "willing" it over long spaces of time.

The curious "optimism" of Nietzsche, by means of which he sought to force himself into a mood of such Dionysian ecstasy as to be able not only to endure Fate, but to "love" it, is yet another example of the subterranean "conscience" of Christianity working in him. In the presence of such a mood, and, indeed, in the presence of nearly all his great dramatic Passions, it is Nietzsche, and not his humorous critic, who is "with Our Lord" in Gethsamene. One does not drink of the cup of Fate "lovingly"—without bloody sweat!

The interesting thing to observe about Nietzsche's ideas is that the wider they depart from what was essentially Christian in him, the less convincing they grow. One cannot help feeling he recognised this himself—and, infuriated by it, strode further and further into the Jungle.

For instance, one cannot suppose that the cult of "the Blonde Beast," and the cult of Caesar Borgia, were anything but mad reprisals, directed towards himself, in savage revenge; blind blows struck at random against the lofty and penetrating spirituality in which he had indulged when writing Zarathustra.

But there is a point here of some curious psychological interest, to which we are attracted by a certain treacherous red glow upon his words when he speaks of this sultry, crouching, spotted, tail-lashing mood. Why is it precisely this Borgian type, this Renaissance type, among the world's various Lust-Darlings that he chooses to select?

Why does he not oppose, to the Christian Ideal, *its true opposite*—the naive, artless, faun-like, pagan "child of Nature," who has never known "remorse"?

The answer is clear. He chooses the Borgian type—the type which is *not* free from "superstition," which is always wrestling with "superstition"—the type that sprinkles holy water upon its dagger—because such a type is the inevitable *product* of the presence among us of the Christian Ideal. The Christian Ideal has made a certain complication of "wickedness" possible, which were impossible without it.

If Nietzsche had not been obsessed by Christianity he would have selected as his "Ideal Blond Beast" that perfectly naive, "unfallen" man, of imperturbable nerves, of classic nerves, such as Life abounded in *before Christ came*. He makes, indeed, a pathetic struggle to idealize this type, rather than the "conscience-striken" Renaissance one. He lets his fingers stray more than once over the red-stained limbs of real sun-burnt "Pompeian" heathenism. He turns feverishly the wanton pages of Petronius to reach this unsullied, "imperial" Animal. But he cannot reach him. He never could reach him. The "consecrated" dagger of the Borgia gleams and scintillates between. Even, therefore, in the sort of "wickedness" he evokes, Nietzsche remains Christ-ridden and Christ-mastered. The matter is made still more certain when one steals up silently, so to speak, behind the passages where he speaks of Napoleon.

If a reader has the remotest psychological clairvoyance, he will be aware of a certain strain and tug, a certain mental jerk and contortion, whenever Napoleon is introduced.

Yes, he could engrave that fatal "N" over his mantlepiece at Weimar—to do so was the last solace of his wounded brain. But he was never really at ease with the great Emperor. Never did he—in pure, direct, classic recognition—greet him as "the Demonic Master of Destiny," with the Goethean salutation! Had Goethe and Napoleon, in their notorious encounter, wherein they recognized one another as "Men," been interrupted by the entrance of Nietzsche, do you suppose they would not have both stiffened and recoiled, recognizing their natural Enemy, the Cross-bearer, the Christ-obsessed one, *"Il Santo"*?

The difference between the two types can best be felt by recalling the way in which Napoleon and Goethe treated the Christ-Legend, compared with Nietzsche's desperate wrestling.

Napoleon uses "Religion" calmly and deliberately for his High Policy and Worldly Statecraft.

Goethe uses "Religion" calmly and deliberately for his aesthetic culture and his mystic symbolism. Neither of them are, for one moment, touched by it themselves.

They are born Pagans; and when this noble, tortured soul flings himself at their feet in feverish worship, one feels that, out of their Homeric Hades, they look wonderingly, *unintelligently,* at him.

One of the most laughable things in the world is the attempt some simple critics make to turn Nietzsche into an ordinary "Honest Infidel," a kind of poetic Bradlaugh-Ingersoll, offering to humanity the profound discovery that there is no God, and that when we die, we die! The absurdity is made complete when this naive, revivified "Pagan" is made to assure us—us, "the average sensual men"—that the path of wisdom lies, not in resisting, but in yielding to *temptation;* not in spiritual wrestling to "transform" ourselves, but in the brute courage "to be ourselves," and "live out our type"!

The good folk who play with such a childish illusion would do well to scan over again their "pagan" hero's branding and flaying of the philosopher Strauss. Strauss was precisely what they try to turn Nietzsche into—a rancorous, insensitive, bullying, materialistic Heathen, making sport of "the Cross" and drinking Laager Beer. Nietzsche loathed Laager Beer, and "the Cross" *burnt* day and night in his tormented, Dionysian soul.

It occurs to me sometimes that if there had been no "German Reformation" and no over-running of the world by vulgar evangelical Protestantism, it would be still possible to bring into the circle of the Church's development the lofty and desperate Passion of this "saintly" Antichrist. After all, why should we concede that those agitated, voluptuous, secret devices to get "saved," those super-subtle, subliminal tricks of the weak and the perverted to be *revenged* on the beautiful and the brave, which Nietzsche laments were ever "bound up" in the same cover as the "Old Testament," must remain forever the dominant "note" in the Faith of Christendom? While the Successor of Caesar, while the Pontifex Maximus of our "Spiritual Rome," still represents the Infallible Element in the world's nobler religious Taste, there is yet, perhaps, a remote

NIETZSCHE

chance that this vulgarizing of "the mountain summits," this degrading of our Planet's Passion-Play, may be cauterized and eliminated.

And yet it is not likely! Much more likely is it that the real "secret" of Jesus, together with the real "secret" of Nietzsche—and they do not differ in essence, for all his Borgias!—will remain the sweet and deadly "fatalities" they have always been—for the few, the few, the few who understand them!

For the final impression one carries away, after reading Nietzsche, is the impression of "distinction," of remoteness from "vulgar brutality," from "sensual baseness," from the clumsy compromises of the world. It may not last, this Zarathustrian mood. It lasts with some of us an hour; with some of us a day—with a few of us a handful of years! But while it lasts, it is a rare and high experience. As from an ice-bound promontory stretching out over the absymal gulfs, we dare to look Creation and Annihilation, for once, full in the face.

Liberated from our own lusts, or using them, contemptuously and indifferently, as engines of vision, we see the life and death of worlds, the slow, long-drawn, moon-lit wave of Universe-drowning Nothingness.

We see the races of men, falling, rising, stumbling, advancing and receding—and we see the *new race*—in the hours of the "Great Noon-tide"—fulfilling its Prophet's hope—and we see *the end of that also!* And seeing all this, because the air of our watch-tower is so ice-cold and keen, we neither tremble or blench. The world is deep, and deep is pain, and deeper than pain is joy. We have seen Creation, and have exulted in it. We have seen Destruction, and have exulted in it. We have watched the long, quivering Shadow of Life shudder across our glacial promontory, and we have watched that drowning tide receive it. It is enough. It is well. We have had our Vision. We know now what gives to the gods "that look" their faces wear.

It now only remains for us to return to the familiar human Stage; to the "Gala-Night, within the lonesome latter years," and be gay, and "hard," and "superficial"!

That ice-bound Promontory into the Truth of Things has only known one Explorer whose "Eloi, Eloi Lama Sabacthani" was not the death-cry of his Pity. And that Explorer—did we only dream of his Return?

THOMAS HARDY

THOMAS HARDY

ITH a name suggestive of the purest English origin, Mr. Hardy has become identified with that portion of England where the various race-deposits in our national "strata" are most clear and defined. In Wessex, the traditions of Saxon and Celt, Norman and Dane, Roman and Iberian, have grown side by side into the soil, and all the villages and towns, all the hills and streams, of this country have preserved the rumour of what they have seen.

In Celtic legend the country of the West Saxons is marvellously rich. Camelot and the Island of Avalon greet one another across the Somersetshire vale. And Dorsetshire, Hardy's immediate home, adds the Roman traditions of Casterbridge to tragic memories of King Lear. Tribe by tribe, race by race, as they come and go, leaving their monuments and their names behind, Mr. Hardy broods over them, noting their survivals, their lingering footprints, their long decline.

In his well-loved Dorchester we find him pondering, like one of his own spirits of Pity and Irony, while the moonlight shines on the haunted amphitheatre where the Romans held their games. He devotes much care to noting all those little "omens by the way" that make a journey along the great highways of Wessex so full of imaginative suggestion.

It is the history of the human race itself that holds him with a mesmeric spell, as century after century it unrolls its acts and scenes, under the indifferent stars. The continuity of life! The long, piteous "ascent of man," from those queer fossils in the Portland Quarries— to what we see today, so palpable, so real! And yet for all his tragic pity, Mr. Hardy is a sly and whimsical chronicler. He does not allow one point of the little jest the gods play on us—the little long-drawn-out jest—to lose its sting. With something of a goblin-like alertness he skips here and there, watching those strange scene shifters at their work. The dual stops of Mr. Hardy's country pipe are cut from the same reed. With the one he challenges the Immortals on behalf of humanity; with the other he plays such a shrewd Priapian tune that all the Satyrs dance.

I sometimes think that only those born and bred in the country can do justice to this great writer. That dual pipe of his is bewildering to city people. They over emphasize the "magnanimity" of his art, or they over emphasize its "miching-mallecho." They do not catch the secret of that mingled strain. The same type of cultured "foreigner" is puzzled by Mr. Hardy's self-possession. He ought to commit himself more completely, or he ought not to have committed himself at all! There is something that looks to them—so they are tempted to express it—like the cloven hoof of a most Satyrish cunning, about his attitude to certain things. That little caustic by-play, for instance, with which he girds at the established order, never denouncing it wholesale like Shelley, or accepting it wholesale like Wordsworth—and always with a tang, a dash of gall and wormwood, an impish malice.

The truth is, there are two spirits in Mr. Hardy, one infinitely sorrowful and tender, the other whimsical, elfish and malign.

The first spirit rises up in stern Promethean revolt against the decrees of Fate. The second spirit deliberately allies itself in wanton, bitter glee, with the humorous provocation of humanity, by the cruel Powers of the Air. The psychology of all this is not hard to unravel. The same abnormal sensitiveness that makes him pity the victims of destiny makes him also not unaware of what may be sweet to the palate of the gods in such "merry jests." These two tendencies seem to have grown upon him as years went on and to have become more and more pronounced. Often, with artists, the reverse thing happens. Every human being has his own secretive reaction, his own furtive recoil, from the queer trap we are all in,—his little private method of retaliation. But many writers are most unscrupulously themselves when they are young. The changes and chances of this mortal life mellow them into a more neutral tint. Their revenge upon life grows less personal and more objective as they get older. They become balanced and resigned. They attain "the wisdom of Sophocles."

The opposite of this has been the history of Mr. Hardy's progression. He began with quite harmless rustic realism, fanciful and quaint. Then came his masterpieces wherein the power and grandeur of a great artist's inspiration fused everything into harmony. At the last, in his third period, we have the exaggeration of all that is most personal in his emotion intensified to the extreme limit.

It is absurd to turn away from these books, books like Jude the Obscure and the Well-Beloved. If Mr. Hardy had not had such sardonic emotions, such desire to "hit back" at the great "opposeless wills," and such Goblin-like glee at the tricks they play us, he would never have been able to write "Tess." Against the ways of God to this sweet girl he raises a hand of terrible revolt, but it is with more than human "pity" that he lays her down on the Altar of Sacrifice.

THOMAS HARDY

But, after all, it is in the supreme passages of pure imaginative grandeur that Mr. Hardy is greatest. Here he is "with Shakespeare," and we forget both Titan and Goblin. How hard it is exactly to put into words what this "imaginative grandeur" consists of! It is, at any rate, an intensification of our general consciousness of the Life-Drama as a whole, but this, under a poetic, rather than a scientific, light, and yet with the scientific facts,—they also not without their dramatic significance—indicated and allowed for. It is a clarifying of our mental vision and a heightening of our sensual apprehension. It is a certain withdrawing from the mere personal pull of our own fate into a more rarified air, where the tragic beauty of life falls into perspective, and, beholding the world in a clear mirror, we escape for a moment from "the will to live."

At such times it is as though, "taken up upon a high mountain, we see, without desire and without despair, the kingdoms of the world and the glories of them." Then it is that we feel the very wind of the earth's revolution, and the circling hours touch us with a palpable hand.

And the turmoil of the world grown so distant, it is then that we feel at once the greatness of humanity and the littleness of what it strives for. We are seized with a shuddering tenderness for Man. This bewildered animal

—wrestling in darkness with he knows not what.

And gazing long and long into this mirror, the poignancy of what we behold is strangely softened. After all, it is something, whatever becomes of us, to have been conscious of all this. It is something to have outwatched Arcturus, and felt "the sweet influences" of the Pleiades. Congruous with such a mood is the manner in which, while Mr. Hardy opposes himself to Christianity, he cannot forget it. He cannot "cleanse the stuff'd bosom of that perilous stuff which weighs upon the heart." It troubles and vexes him. It haunts him. And his work both gains and suffers. He flings gibe after gibe at "God," but across his anger falls the shadow of the Cross. How should it not be so? "All may be permitted," but one must not add a feather's weight to the wheel that breaks our "little ones."

It is this that separates Mr. Hardy's work from so much modern fiction that is clever and "philosophical" but does not satisfy one's imagination. All things with Mr. Hardy—even the facts of geology and chemistry—are treated with that imaginative clairvoyance that gives them their place in the human comedy. And is not Christianity itself one of these facts? How amazing that such a thing should have appeared at all upon the earth! When one reads Meredith, with his brilliant intellectual cleverness, one finds Christianity "taken for granted," and dismissed as hardly relevant to modern topics.

But Mr. Hardy is too pagan, in the true sense, too fascinated by the poetry of life and the essential ritual of life, to dismiss any great religion in this way. The thing is always with him, just as the Gothic Tower of St. Peter's Church in Casterbridge is always with him. He may burst into impish fury with its doctrines, but, like one of those queer demons who peep out from such consecrated places, yet never leave them, his imagination requires that atmosphere. For the same reason, in spite of his intellectual realization of the mechanical processes of Fate, their engine-like dumbness and blindness, he is always being driven to *personify* these ultimate powers; to personify them, or *it,* as something that takes infernal satisfaction in fooling its luckless creations; in provoking them and scourging them to madness.

Mr. Hardy's ultimate thought is that the universe is blind and unconscious; that it knows not what it does. But, standing among the graves of those Wessex churchyards, or watching the twisted threads of perverse destiny that plague those hapless hearts under a thousand village roofs, it is impossible for him not to long to "strike back" at this damned System of Things that alone is responsible.

VISIONS AND REVISIONS

And how can one "strike back" unless one converts unconscious machinery into a wanton Providence? Where Mr. Hardy is so incomparably greater than Meredith and all his modern followers is that in these Wessex novels there is none of that intolerable "ethical discussion" which obscures "the old essential candours" of the human situation.

The reaction of men and women upon one another, in the presence of the solemn and the mocking elements; this will outlast all social readjustments and all ethical reforms.

While the sun shines and the moon draws the tides, men and women will ache from jealousy, and the lover will not be the beloved! Long after a quite new set of "interesting modern ideas" have replaced the present, children will break the hearts of their parents, and parents will break the hearts of their children. Mr. Hardy is indignant enough over the ridiculous conventions of Society, but he knows that, at the bottom, what we suffer from is "the dust out of which we are made;" the eternal illusion and disillusion which must drive us on and "take us off" until the planet's last hour.

Mr. Hardy's style, at its best, has an imaginative suggestiveness which approaches, though it may not quite reach, the indescribable touch of the Shakespearean tragedies. There is also a quality in it peculiar to himself —threatening and silencing; a thunderous suppression, a formidable reserve, an iron tenacity. Sometimes, again, one is reminded of the ancient Roman poets, and not unfrequently, too, of the rhymmic incantations of Sir Thomas Browne, that majestic and perverted Latinist.

The description, for instance, of Egdon Heath, at the beginning of the Return of the Native, has a dusky architectural grandeur that is like the Portico of an Egyptian Temple. The same thing may be noted of that sudden apparition of Stonehenge, as Tess and Angel stumble upon it in their flight through the darkness.

One thinks of the words of William Blake: "He who does not love Form more than Colour is a coward." For it is, above all, Form that appeals to Mr. Hardy. The iron plough of his implacable style drives pitilessly through the soft flesh of the earth until it reaches the architectural sub-structure. Whoever tries to visualize any scene out of the Wessex Novels will be forced to see the figures of the persons concerned "silhouetted" against a formidable skyline. One sees them, these poor impassioned ones, moving in tragic procession along the edge of the world, and, when the procession is over, darkness re-establishes itself. The quality that makes Mr. Hardy's manner such a refuge from the levities and gravities of the "reforming writers" is a quality that springs from the soil. The soil has a gift of "proportion" like nothing else. Things fall into due perspective on Egdon Heath, and among the water-meadows of Blackmoor life is felt as the tribes of men have felt it since the beginning.

The modern tendency is to mock at sexual passion and grow grave over social and artistic problems. Mr. Hardy eliminates social and artistic problems and "takes nothing seriously" —not even "God"—except the love and the hate of men and women, and the natural elements that are their accomplices. It is for this lack in them, this uneasy levity over the one thing that really counts, that it is so hard to read many humorous and arresting modern writers, except in railway trains and cafés. They have thought it clever to dispossess the passion of our poor heart of its essential poetry. They have not understood that man would sooner suffer the bitterness of death than be deprived of his *right* to suffer the bitterness of love.

It must be, I suppose, that these flippant triflers are so optimistic about their reforms and their ethical ideals and their sanitary projects that to them such things as how the sun rises over Shaston and sinks over Budmouth; such things as what Eustacia felt when she walked, "talking to herself," across the blasted heath; such things as the mood of Henchard when he cursed the day of his birth, are mere accidents and irrelevancies, by no means germane to the matter.

Well, perhaps they are wise to be so hopeful. But for the rest of us, for whom the world does not seem likely to "improve" so fast, it is an unspeakable relief that there should be at least one writer left interested in the things that interested Sophocles and Shakespeare, and possessed of a style that does not, remembering the work of such hands, put our generation altogether to shame.

WALTER PATER

WALTER PATER

HAT are the qualities that make this shy and furtive Recluse, this Wanderer in the shadow, the greatest of critics? Imagination, in the first place, and then that rare, unusual, divine gift of limitless Reverence for the Human Senses. Imagination has a two-fold power. It visualizes and it creates. With clairvoyant ubiquity it floats and flows into the most recondite recesses, the most reluctant sanctuaries, of other men's souls. With clear-cut, architectural volition it builds up its own Byzantium, out of the quarried débris of all the centuries.

One loves to think of Pater leaving that Olney country, where he "hated" to hear anything more about "the Poet Cowper," and nursing his weird boy-fancies in the security of the Canterbury cloisters. The most passionate and dedicated spirit he—to sulk, and dream, and hide, and love, and "watch the others playing," in that quiet retreat—since the great soul of Christopher Marlowe flamed up there into consciousness!

And then Oxford. And it is meet and right,

at such a point as this, to lay our offering, modest, secret, shy—a shadow, a nothing—at the feet of this gracious Alma Mater; "who needs not June for Beauty's heightening!" One revolts against her sometimes. The charm is too exclusive, too withdrawn. And something—what shall I say?—of ironic, supercilious disillusion makes her forehead weary, and her eyelids heavy. But after all, to what exquisite children, like rare, exotic flowers, she has the power to give birth! But did you know, you for whom the syllables "Oxford" are an Incantation, that to the yet more subtle, yet more withdrawn, and yet more elaborate soul of Walter Pater, Oxford Herself appeared, as time went on, a little vulgar and silly?

Indeed, he fled from her, and took refuge—sometimes with his sisters, for, like Charles Lamb, Pater was "Conventual" in his taste—and sometimes with the "original" of Marius the Epicurean. But what matter where he fled—he who always followed the "shady side" of the road? He has not only managed to escape, himself, with all his "Boxes of Alabaster," into the sanctuary of the Ivory Tower, that even Oxford cannot reach, but he has carried us thither with him.

And there, from the opal-clouded windows of that high place, he shows us still the secret kingdoms of art and philosophy and life, and the remotest glories of them. We see them all—from those windows—a little lovelier, a little rarer, a little more "selective," than, perchance, they really are. But what matter? What does one expect when one looks through opal-clouded windows? And, after all, those are the kinds of windows from which it is best to look at the dazzling limbs of the immortal gods!

Not but what, sometimes, he permits us to throw those "magic casements" wide open. And then, in how lucid an air, in how clean and fresh a morning of reality, those pure forms and godlike figures stand out, their naked feet in the cold, clear dew!

For one must note two things about Walter Pater. He is able to throw the glimmering mantle of his own elaborate *sophistry of the senses* over comparatively fleeting, unarresting objects. And he is able to compel us to follow, line by line, curve by curve, contour by contour, the very palpable body and presence of the Beauty that passeth not away.

In plainer words, he is a great and exact scholar—laborious, patient, indefatigable, reserved; and, at the same time, a Protean Wizard, breathing forbidden life into the Tyrian-stained writhings of many an enchanted Lamia! At a thousand points he is the only modern literary figure who draws us towards him with the old Leonardian, Goethean spell For, like Goethe and Da Vinci, he is never far from those eternal "Partings of the Ways," which alone make life interesting.

He is, for instance, more profoundly drenched, dyed, and endued in "Christian Mythology" than any mortal writer, short of the Saints themselves. He is more native to the pure Hellenic air than any since Walter Savage Landor. And he is more subtle, in his understanding of "German Philosophy" as opposed to "Celtic Romance," than all—outside the most inner circles—since Hegel—or Heine! The greedy, capricious "Uranian Babyishness" of his pupil Oscar, with its peevish clutching at all soft and provocative and glimmering things, is mere child's play, compared with the deep, dark Vampirism with which this furtive Hermit drains the scarlet blood of the Vestals of every Sanctuary.

How little the conventional critics have understood this master of their own craft! What hopeless people have "rushed in" to interpret this super-subtle Interpreter! Mr. Gosse has, however, done one thing for us. Somewhere, somehow, he once drew a picture of Walter Pater "gambolling," in the moonlight, on the velvet lawn of his own secluded Oxford garden, like a satin-pawed Wombat! I always think of that picture. It is a pleasanter one than that of Mark Pattison, running round his Gooseberry bushes, after great screaming girls. But they are both touching sketches, and, no doubt, very indicative of Life beneath the shadow of the Bodleian.

Why have the professional philosophers—ever since that Master of Baliol who used to spend his time boring holes in the Ship that carried him—"fought shy" of Pater's Philosophy? For a sufficient reason! Because, like Protagoras the Sophist, and like Aristippus the Cyrenean, he has undermined Metaphysic, *by means of Metaphysic*.

For Walter Pater—is that clearly understood?—was an adept, long before Nietzsche's campaign began, at showing the human desire, the human craving, the human ferocity, the human spite, hidden behind the mask of "Pure Reason."

He treats every great System of Metaphysic as a great work of Art—with a very human, often a too human, artizan behind it—a work of Art which we have a perfect right to appropriate, to enjoy, to look at the world through, and then *to pass on!*

Every Philosophy has its "secret," according to Pater, its "formula," its lost Atlantis. Well! It is for us to search it out; to take colour from its dim-lit under-world; to feed upon its wavering Sea-Lotus—and then, returning to the surface, to swim away, in search of other diving-grounds!

No Philosopher except Pater has dared to carry Esoteric Eclecticism quite as far as this.

And, be it understood, he is no frivolous Dilettante. This draining the secret wine of the great embalmed Sarcophagi of Thought is his Life-Lure, his secret madness, his grand obsession. Walter Pater approaches a System of Metaphysical Thought as a somewhat furtive amorist might approach a sleeping Nymph. On light-stepping, crafty feet he approaches—and the hand with which he twitches the sleeve of the sleeper is as soft as the flutter of a moth's wing. "I do not like," he said once, "to be called a Hedonist. It gives such a queer impression to people who don't know Greek."

Ardent young people sometimes come to me, when in the wayfaring of my patient academic duties, I speak about Pater, and ask me pointblank to tell them what his "view-point"—so they are pleased to express it—"really and truly" was. Sweet reader, do you know the pain of these "really and truly" questions? I try to answer in some blundering manner like this. I try to explain how, for him, nothing in this world was certain or fixed; how everything "flowed away"; how all that we touch or taste or see, vanished, changed its nature, became something else, even as we vanish, as the years go on, and change our nature and become something else. I try to explain how, for him, we are ourselves but the meeting-places of strange forces, journeying at large and by chance through a shifting world; how we, too, these very meeting-places of such forces, waver and flicker and shift and are transformed, like dreams within dreams!

I try to explain how, this being so, and nothing being "written in the sky," it is our right to test every single experience that life can offer, short of those which would make things bitterer, harder, narrower, less easy, for "the other person."

And if my Innocents ask—as they do sometimes—Innocents are like that!—"Why must we consider the other person?" I answer—for no *reason,* and under no threat or danger or categorical imperative; but simply because we have grown to be the sort of animal, the sort of queer fish, who *cannot* do the things "that he would"! It is not, I try to indicate, a case of conscience; it is a matter of taste; and there are certain things, when it comes to that point, which an animal possessed of such taste *cannot do,* even though he desire to do them. And one of these things is to hurt the other trapped creatures who happen to have been caught in the same "gin" as ourself.

With regard to Art and Literature, Pater has the same method as with regard to Philosophy. Everything in a world so fluid is obviously relative. It is ridiculous to dream that there is any absolute standard—even of beauty itself. Those high and immutable Principles of The Good and True are as much an illusion as any other human dream. There are no such principles. Beauty is a Daughter of Life, and is forever changing as Life changes, and as we change who have to live. The lonely, tragic faith of certain great souls in that high, cold "Mathematic" of the Universe, the rhythm of whose ordered Harmony is the Music of the Spheres, is a Faith that may well inspire and solemnize us; it cannot persuade or convince us.

Beauty is not Mathematical; it is—if one may say so—physiological and psychological, and though that austere severity of pure line and pure color, the impersonal technique of art, has a seemingly pre-ordained power of appeal, in reality it is far less immutable than it appears, and has far more in it of the arbitrariness of life and growth and change than we sometimes would care to allow.

Walter Pater's magnetic spell is never more wonder-working than when he deals with the *materials* which artists use. And most of all, with *words,* that material which is so stained and corrupted and outraged—and yet which is the richest of all. But how tenderly he always speaks of materials! What a 'mitless reverence he has for the subtle reciprocity and correspondence between the human senses and what —so thrillingly, so dangerously, sometimes!— they apprehend. Wood and clay and marble and bronze and gold and silver; these—and the fabrics of cunning looms and deft, insatiable fingers—he handles with the reverence of a priest touching consecrated elements.

Not only the great main rivers of art's tradition, but the little streams and tributaries, he loves. Perhaps he loves some of these best of all, for the pathways to their exquisite margins are less trodden than the others, and one is more apt to find one's self alone there.

Perhaps of all his essays, three might be selected as most characteristic of certain recurrent moods. That one on Denys L'Auxerrois, where the sweet, perilous legend of the exiled god—has he really been ever far from us, that treacherous Son of scorched white Flesh?—leads us so far, so strangely far. That one on Watteau, the Prince of Court Painters, where his passion for things faded and withdrawn reaches its climax. For Pater, like Antoine, is one of those always ready to turn a little wearily from the pressure of their own too vivid days, and seek a wistful escape in some fantastic valley of dreams. Watteau's "happy valley" is, indeed, sadder than our most crowded hours—how should it not be, when it is no "valley" at all, but the melancholy cypress-alleys of Versailles?—but, though sadder, it is so fine; so fine and rare and gay!

And along the borders of it and under its clipped trees, by its fountains and ghostly lawns, still, still can one catch in the twilight the shimmer of the dancing feet of the Phantom-Pierrot, and the despair in his smile! For him, too—for Gilles the Mummer—as for Antoine Watteau and Walter Pater, the wistfulness of such places is not inconsistent with their levity. Soon the music must stop. Soon it must be only a garden, "only a garden of Lenotre, correct, ridiculous and charming." For the lips of the Despair of Pierrot cannot always touch the lips of the Mockery of Columbine; in the end, the Ultimate Futility must turn them both to stone!

And, finally, that Essay upon Leonardo, with the lines "we say to our friend," about Her who is "older than the rocks on which she sits."

What really makes Pater so great, so wise, so salutary a writer is his perpetual insistence on the criminal, mad foolishness of letting slip, in silly chatter and vapid preaching, the unreturning days of our youth! "Carry, O Youths and Maidens," he seems to say. "Carry with infinite devotion that vase of many odours which is your Life on Earth. Spill as little as may be of its unvalued wine; let no rain-drops or bryony-dew, or floating gossamer-seed, fall into it and spoil its taste. For it is all you have, and it cannot last long!

He is a great writer, because from him we may learn the difficult and subtle art of drinking the cup of life *so as to taste every drop.*

WALTER PATER

One could expatiate long upon his attitude to Christianity—his final desire to be "ordained Priest"—his alternating pieties and incredulities. His deliberate clinging to what "experience" brought him, as the final test of "truth," made it quite easy for him to dip his arms deep into the Holy Well. He might not find the Graal; he might see nothing there but his own shadow! What matter? The Well itself was so cool and chaste and dark and cavern-like, that it was worth long summer days spent dreaming over it—dreaming over it in the cloistered garden, out of the dust and the folly and the grossness of the brutal World, that knows neither Apollo or Christ!

DOSTOIEVSKY

DOSTOIEVSKY

HE first discovery of Dostoievsky is, for a spiritual adventurer, such a shock as is not likely to occur again. One is staggered, bewildered, insulted. It is like a hit in the face, at the end of a dark passage; a hit in the face, followed by the fumbling of strange hands at one's throat. Everything that has been *forbidden,* by discretion, by caution, by self-respect, by atavistic inhibition, seems suddenly to leap up out of the darkness and seize upon one with fierce, indescribable caresses.

All that one has *felt,* but has not dared to think; all that one has *thought,* but has not dared to say; all the terrible whispers from the unspeakable margins; all the horrible wreckage and silt from the unsounded depths, float in upon us and overpower us.

There is so much that the other writers, even the realists among them, cannot, *will* not, say. There is so much that the normal self-preservative instincts in ourselves do not *want* said. But this Russian has no mercy. Such exposures humiliate and disgrace? What matter? It is well that we should be so laid bare. Such revelations provoke and embarrass? What matter? We *require* embarrassment. The quicksilver of human consciousness must have no closed chinks, no blind alleys. It must be compelled to reform its microcosmic reflections, even *down there,* where it has to be driven by force. It is extraordinary how superficial even the great writers are; how lacking in the Mole's claws, in the Woodpecker's beak! They seem labouring beneath some pathetic vow, exacted by the Demons of our Fate, under terrible threats, only to reveal what will serve *their* purpose! This applies as much to the Realists, with their traditional animal chemistry, as to the Idealists, with their traditional ethical dynamics. It applies, above all, to the interpreters of Sex, who, in their conventional grossness, as well as in their conventional discretion, bury such Ostrich heads in the sand!

The lucky-unlucky individual whose path this formidable writer crosses, quickly begins, as he reads page by page, to cry out in startled wonder, in terrified protest. This rending Night Hawk reveals just what one hugged most closely of all—just what one did *not* confess! Such a person, reading this desperate "clairvoyant," finds himself laughing and chuckling, under his breath, and *against his will,* over the little things there betrayed. It is not any more a case of enjoying with distant aesthetic amusement the general human spectacle. He himself is the one scratched and pricked. He himself is the one so abominably tickled. That is why women—who have so mad a craving for the personal in everything—are especially caught by Dostoievsky. He knows them so fatally well. Those startling, contradictory feelings that make their capricious bosoms rise and fall, those feelings that they find so difficult themselves to understand, he drags them all into the light. The kind of delicate cruelty, that in others becomes something worse, refines itself in his magnetic genius into a cruelty of insight that knows no scruple. Nor is the reluctance of these gentle beings, so thrillingly betrayed, to yield their passionate secrets, unaccompanied by pleasure. They suffer to feel themselves so exposed, but it is an exquisite suffering. It may, indeed, be said that the strange throb of satisfaction with which we human beings feel ourselves *at the bottom,* where we cannot fall lower, or be further unmasked, is never more frequent than when we read Dostoievsky. And that is largely because he alone understands *the depravity of the spirit,* as well as of the flesh, and the amazing wantonness, whereby the human will does not always seek its own realization and well-being, but quite as often its own laceration and destruction.

VISIONS AND REVISIONS

Dostoievsky has, indeed, a demonic power of revelation in regard to that twilight of the human brain, where lurk the phantoms of unsatisfied desire, and where unspoken lusts stretch forth pitiable hands. There are certain human experiences which the conventional machinery of ordinary novel-writing lacks all language to express. He expresses these, not in tedious analysis, but in the living cries, and gasps, and gestures, and fumblings and silences of his characters themselves. Who, like Dostoievsky, has shown the tragic association of passionate love with passionate hate, which is so frequent a human experience?

This monstrous *hate-love,* caressing the bruises itself has made, and shooting forth a forked viper-tongue of cruelty from between the lips that kiss—has anyone but he held it fast, through all its Protean changes? I suppose, when one really thinks of it, at the bottom of every one of us lurk two *primary emotions*—vanity and fear. It is in their knowledge of the aberrations of these, of the mad contortions that these lead to, that the other writers seem so especially simple-minded. Over and over again, in reading Dostoievsky, one is positively seized by the throat with astonishment at the man's insight into the labyrinthian retreats of our secret pride—and of our secret fear. His characters, at certain moments, seem actually to spit gall and wormwood, as they tug at the quivering roots of one another's self-esteem. But this fermenting venom, this seething scum, is only the expression of what goes on below the surface every day, in every country.

Dostoievsky's Russians are cruelly voluble, but their volubility taps the evil humour of the universal human disease. Their thoughts are *our* thoughts, their obsessions, *our* obsessions. Let no one think, in his vain security, that he has a right to say: "I have no part in this morbidity. I am different from these poor madmen."

The curious nervous relief we experience as we read these books is alone a sufficient vindication. They relieve us, as well as trouble us, because in these pages we all confess what we have never confessed to anyone. Our self-love is outraged, but outraged with that strange accompaniment of thrilling pleasure that means an expiation paid, a burden lightened. Use the word "degenerate" if you will. But in this sense we are all "degenerates," for thus and not otherwise is woven the stuff whereof men are made.

Certainly the Russian soul has its peculiarities, and these peculiarities we feel in Dostoievsky as nowhere else. He, not Tolstoi or Turgenieff, is the typical Slav writer. But the chief peculiarity of the Russian soul is that it is not ashamed to express what all men feel.

And this is why Dostoievsky is not only a Russian writer but a universal writer. From the French point of view he may seem wanting in lucidity and irony; from the English point of view he may seem antinomian and non-moral. But he has one advantage over both. He approaches the ultimate mystery as no Western writer, except, perhaps, Shakespeare and Goethe, has ever approached it. He writes with human nerves upon parchment made of human tissue, and "abyssum evocat abyssum," from the darkness wherein he moves.

Among other things, Dostoievsky's insight is proved by the profound separation he indicates between "morality" and "religion." To many of us it comes with something of a shock to find harlots and murderers and robbers and drunkards and seducers and idiots expressing genuine and passionate religious faith, and discussing with desperate interest religious questions. But it is *our* psychology that is shallow and inhuman, not his, and the presence of real religious feeling in a nature obsessed with the maddest lusts is a phenomenon of universal experience. It may, indeed, be said that what is most characteristically Russian in his point of view—he has told us so himself—is the substitution of what might be called "sanctity" for what is usually termed "morality," as an ideal of life. The "Christianity" of which Dostoievsky has the key is nothing if not an ecstatic invasion of regions where ordinary moral laws, based upon prudence and self-preservation, disappear, and give place to something else. The secret of it, beyond repentance and remorse, lies in the transforming power of "love;" lies, in fact, in "vision" purged by pity and terror; but its precise nature is rather to be felt than described.

It is in connection with this Christianity of his, a Christianity completely different from what we are accustomed to, that we find the explanation of his extraordinary interest in the "weak" as opposed to the "strong." The association between Christianity and a certain masterful, moral, self-assertive energy, such as we feel the presence of in England and America, might well tend to make it difficult for us to understand his meaning. It is precisely this sort of thing that makes it difficult for us to understand Russia and the Russian religion.

But as one reads Dostoievsky it is impossible to escape a suspicion that we Western nations have as yet only touched the fringe of what the Christian Faith is capable of, whether considered as a cosmic secret or as a Nepenthe for human suffering.

He saw, with clairvoyant distinctness, how large a part of the impetus of life's movement proceeds from the mad struggle, always going on, between the strong and the weak. It was his emphasis upon this struggle that helped Nietzsche to those withering exposures of "the tyranny of the weak" which cleared the path for his terrific transvaluations. It was Dostoievsky's demonic insight into the pathological sub-soil of the Religion of Pity which helped Nietzsche to forge his flashing counterblasts, but though their vision of the "general situation" thus coincided, their conclusions were diametrically different. For Nietzsche the hope of humanity is found in the strong; for Dostoievsky it is found in the weak. Their only ground of agreement is that they both refute the insolent claims of mediocrity and normality.

One of the most arresting "truths" that emerge, like silvery fish, at the end of the line of this Fisher in the abysses is the "truth" that any kind of departure from the Normal may become a means of mystic illumination. The same perversion or contortion of mind which may, in one direction, lead to crime may, in another direction, lead to extraordinary spiritual clairvoyance. And this applies to *all* deviations from the normal type, and to all moods and inclinations in normal persons under unusual excitement or strain. The theory is, as a matter of fact, as old as the oldest races. In Egypt and India, as well as in Rome and Athens, the gods were always regarded as in some especial way manifesting their will, and revealing their secrets, to those thus stricken. The view that wisdom is attained along the path of normal health and rational sanity has always been a "philosophical" and never a "religious" view. Dostoievsky's dominant idea has, indeed, many affinities with the Pauline one, and is certainly a quite justifiable derivation from the Evangelical doctrine. It is, however, none the less startling to our Western mind.

In Dostoievsky's books, madmen, idiots, drunkards, consumptives, degenerates, visionaries, reactionaries, anarchists, nympholepts, criminals and saints jostle one another in a sort of "Danse Macabre," but not one of them but has his moment of ecstasy. The very worst of them, that little band of fantastic super-men of lust, whose extravagant manias and excesses of remorse suggest attitudes and gestures that would need an Aubrey Beardsley for illustration, have, at moments, moods of divine sublimity. Nikolay Vsyevolodovitch Stavrogin, in "the Possessed;" Svridigilaiof Dounia's would-be seducer, in "Crime and Punishment," and Ivan, in "the Brothers Karamazov," though all inspired by ten thousand demons, cannot be called devoid of a certain mysterious spiritual greatness. Perhaps the interesting thing about them is that their elaborate wickedness is itself a *spiritual* rather than a *sensual* quality, or, to put it in another way, there are abysmal depths of spiritual subtlety in their most sensual obsession. The only entirely *base* criminal I can recall in Dostoievsky is Stavrogin's admirer, Peter Stepanovitch, and he is transformed and transfigured at times by the sheer intensity of his worship for his friend. It would be overpowering the reader with names, themselves like ritualistic incantations, to enumerate all the perverts and abnormalists whose various lapses and diseases become, in these books, mediums of spiritual insight. Though dealing continually with every form of tragedy and misery, Dostoievsky cannot be called a Pessimist. He is so profoundly affected by the spirit of the Evangelical "Beatitudes" that for him "poverty" and "meekness" and "hungering and thirsting" and "weeping and mourning" are always in the true sense "blessed"—that is to say, they are the path of initiation, the sorrowful gates to the unspeakable joy.

The most beautiful characters he has drawn are, perhaps, Alyosha Karamazov and Prince Myshkin; both of these being young men, and both of them so Christ-like, that in reading about them one is compelled to acknowledge that something in the temper of that Figure, hitherto concealed from His followers, has been communicated to this Russian. The naive, and yet ironical, artlessness of their retorts to the aggressive Philistines who surround them remind one over and over again of those Divine "bon-mots" with which, to use Oscar Wilde's allusion, the Redeemer bewildered His assailants. Stephan Trophinovitch reading the Miracle of the Swine with his female Colporteur; Raskolnikoff reading the Miracle of the Raising of Lazarus with his prostitute Sonia, are scenes that might strike an English mind as mere melodramatic sentiment, but those who have entered into the Dostoievsky secret know how much more than that there is in them, and how deep into the mystery of things and the irony of things they go. One is continually coming upon passages in Dostoievsky the strange and ambiguous nature of which leads one's thought far enough from Evangelical simplicities; passages that are, indeed, at once so beautiful and so sinister that they make one think of certain demonic sayings of Goethe or Spinoza; and yet even these passages do no more than throw new and formidable light upon the "old situations," the old "cross-roads." Dostoievsky is not content with indicating how weakness and disease and suffering can become organs of vision; he goes very far—further than anyone—in his recognition of the secret and perverted cruelty that drives certain persons on to lacerate themselves with all manner of spiritual flagellation.

He understands, better than anyone else, how absurd the philosophical utilitarians are with their axiom that everyone pursues his own happiness. He exposes over and over again, with nerve-rending subtlety, how intoxicating to the human spirit is the mad lust of self-immolation, of self-destruction. It is really from him that Nietzsche learnt that wanton Dionysic talisman which opens the door to such singular spiritual orgies.

Nothing is more characteristic of Dostoievsky's method than his perpetual insistance upon the mania which certain curious human types display for "making fools of themselves." The more sacred aspects of this deliberate self-humiliation require no comment. It is obviously good for our spirit's salvation to be made Fools in Christ. What one has to observe further, under his guidance, is the strange passion that certain derelicts in the human vortex have for being trampled upon and flouted. These queer people—but there are more of them than one would suppose—derive an almost sensual pleasure from being abominably treated. They positively lick the dust before their persecutors. They run to "kiss the rod." It is this type of person who, like the hero in that story in "L'Esprit Souterrain," deliberately rushes into embarrassing situations; into situations and among people where he will look a fool—in order to avenge himself upon the spectators of his "folly" by going deeper and deeper into it.

DOSTOIEVSKY

If Dostoievsky astounds us by his insight into the abnormalities of "normal" men, he is still more startling when he deals with women. There are certain scenes—the scene between Aglaia and Nastasya in "The Idiot;" the scene between Sonia and the mother and sister of Raskolnikoff in "Crime and Punishment;" the scene in "The Possessed" where Liza leaves Stavrogin on the morning after the fire; and the scene where the woman, loved by the mad Karamazov brothers, tears her nerves and theirs to pieces, in outrageous obliquity—which brand themselves upon the mind as reaching the uttermost limit of devasting vision.

In reviewing the final impression left upon one by the reading of Dostoievsky one must confess to many curious reactions. He certainly has the power of making all other novelists seem dull in comparison; dull—or artistic and rhetorical. Perhaps the most marked effect he has is to leave one with the feeling of a universe *with many doors;* with many doors, and not a few terrifyingly dark passages; but a universe the opposite of "closed" or "explained." Though not a single one of his books ends "happily," the final impression is the reverse of hopeless. His very mania for tragedy, his Dionysic embracing of it, precludes any premature despair. Perhaps a profound deepening of one's sense of the mysterious *perversity* of all human fate is the thing that lingers, a perversity which is itself a kind of redemption, for it implies arbitrariness and waywardness, and these things mean power and pleasure, even in the midst of suffering.

He is the best possible antidote for the peculiar and paralysing fatalism of our time, a fatalism which makes so much of "environment" and so little of "character," and which tends to endow mere worldly and material success with a sort of divine prerogative. A generation that allows itself to be even *interested* in such types as the "strong," efficient craftsmen of modern industry and finance is a generation that can well afford a few moral shocks at the hands of Dostoievsky's "degenerates." The world he reveals is, after all, in spite of the Russian names, the world of ordinary human obliquity. The thing for which we have to thank him is that it is made so rich and deep, so full of fathomless pits and unending vistas.

Every great writer brings his own gift, and if others satisfy our craving for destruction and beauty, and yet others our longing for simplification and rational form, the suggestions he brings of mystery and passion, of secret despairs and occult ecstasies, of strange renunciations and stranger triumphs, are such as must quicken our sense of the whole weird game. Looking back over these astonishing books, it is curious to note the impression left of Dostoievsky's feeling for "Nature." No writer one has met with has less of that tendency to "describe scenery," which is so tedious an aspect of most modern work. And yet Russian scenery, and Russian weather, too, seem somehow, without our being aware of it, to have got installed in our brains. Dostoievsky does it incidentally, by innumerable little side-touches and passing allusions, but the general effect remains in one's mind with extraordinary intimacy. The great Russian cities in Summer and Winter, their bridges, rivers, squares, and crowded tenements; the quaint Provincial towns and wayside villages; the desolate outskirts of half-deserted suburbs; and, beyond them all, the feeling of the vast, melancholy plains, crossed by lonely roads; such things, associated in detail after detail with the passions or sorrows of the persons involved, recur as inveterately to the memory as the scenes and weather of our own personal adventures. It is not the self-conscious *art* of a Loti or a D'Annunzio; it is that much more penetrating and imaginative *suggestiveness* which arrests us by its vague beauty and terror in Lear or Macbeth. This subtle inter-penetration between humanity and the familiar Stage of its "exits and entrances" is only one portion of the weight of "cosmic" destiny— one can use no other word—which bears so heavily upon us as we read these books. In other writers one feels that when one has gone "full circle" with the principal characters, and has noted the "descriptive setting," all has been done. Here, as in Aeschylus and Euripides, as in Shakespeare and Goethe, one is left with an intimation of the clash of forces beyond and below humanity, beyond and below nature. One stands at the brink of things unspoken and unspeakable. One "sees the children sport upon the shore, and hears the mighty waters rolling evermore."

In ordinary life we are led, and rightly led —what else can we do?—this way and that by personal feeling and taste and experience. We fight for Religion or fight against Religion. We fight for Morality or fight against Morality. We are Traditionalists or Rebels, Reactionaries or Revolutionaries. Only sometimes, in the fury of our Faith and our Un-Faith, there come, blown across the world-margins, whispers and hints of undreamed of secrets, of unformulated hopes. Then it is that the faces of the people and things we know grow strange and distant, or yield their place to faces we know not and things "lighter than air." Then it is that the most real seems the most dream-like, and the most impossible the most true, for the flowing of the waters of Life have fallen into a new rhythm, and even the children of Saturn may lift up their hearts!

DOSTOIEVSKY

It is too fatally easy, in these days, when machinery—that "Star called Wormwood"—dominates the world, to fall into a state of hard and flippant cynicism, or into a yet more hopeless and weary irony. The unintelligent cheerfulness of the crowd so sickens one; the disingenuous sophistry of its hired preachers fills one with such blank depression that it seems sometimes as though the only mood worthy of normal intelligence were the mood of callous indifference and universal mockery.

All men are liars, and "the Ultimate Futility" grins horribly from its mask. Well! It is precisely at these hours, at the hours when the little pincers of the gods especially nip and squeeze, that it is good to turn the pages of Fyodor Dostoievsky. He brings us his "Balm of Gilead" between the hands of strange people, but it is a true "alabaster box of precious ointment," and though the flowers it contains are snatched from the House of the Dead, one knows at whose feet it was once poured forth, and for whose sake it was broken!

The books that are the most valuable in this world are not the books that pretend to solve life's mystery with a system. They are the books which create a certain mood, a certain temper—the mood, in fact, which is prepared for incredible surprises—the temper which no surprise can overpower. These books of Dostoievsky must always take their place in this great roll, because, though he arrives at no conclusion and utters no oracle, the atmosphere he throws round us is the atmosphere in which Life and Death are "equal;" the gestures his people make, in their great darkness, are the gestures of *that which goes upon its way,* beyond Good and beyond Evil!

Dostoievsky is more than an artist. He is, perhaps—who can tell?—the founder of a new religion. And yet the religion he "founds" is a religion which has been about us for more years than human history can count. He, more than anyone, makes palpable and near—too palpable—O Christ! The terror of it!—that shadowy, monstrous weight of oppressive darkness, through which we signal to each other from our separate Hells. *It* sways and wavers, it gathers and re-gathers, it thickens and deepens, it lifts and sinks, and we know all the while that it is the Thing we ourselves have made, and the intolerable whispers whereof it is full are the children of our own thoughts, of our lusts, of our fears, of our terrible creative dreams.

Dostoievsky's books seem, as one handles them, to flow mysteriously together into one book, and this book is the book of the Last Judgment. The great obscure Land he leads us over, so full of desolate marshes, and forlorn spaces, and hemlock-roots, and drowned tree-trunks, and Golgothas of broken shards and unutterable refuse, is the Land of those visions which are our inmost selves, and for which we are *answerable* and none else.

Across this Land we wander, feeling for some fingers, cold and dead as our own, to share that terror with, and, it may be, finding none, for as we have groped forward we have been pitiless in the darkness, and, half-dead ourselves, have trodden the dead down, and the dead are those who cannot forgive; for murdered "love" has no heart wherewith it should forgive:—*Will the Christ never come?*

EDGAR ALLEN POE

EDGAR ALLEN POE

NE does not feel, by any means, that the last word has been uttered upon this great artist. Has attention been called, for instance, to the sardonic cynicism which underlies his most thrilling effects? Poe's cynicism is itself a very fascinating pathological subject. It is an elaborate thing, compounded of many strange elements. There is a certain dark, wilful melancholy in it that turns with loathing from all human comfort. There is also contempt in it, and savage derision. There is also in it a quality of mood that I prefer to call *Saturnian*—the mood of those born under the planet Saturn. There is cruelty in it, too, and voluptuous cruelty, though cold, reserved, and evasive. It is this "cynicism" of his which makes it possible for him to introduce into his poetry—it is of his poetry that I wish to speak—a certain colloquial salt, pungent and acrid, and with the smell of the tomb about it. It is colloquialism; but it is such colloquialism as ghosts or vampires would use.

Poe remains—that has been already said,

has it not?—absolutely cold while he produces his effects. There is a frozen contempt indicated in every line he writes for the poor facile artists "who speak with tears." Yet the moods through which his Annabels and Ligeias and Ulalumes lead us are moods he must surely himself have known. Yes, he knew them; but they were, so to speak, so completely the atmosphere he lived in that there was no need for him to be carried out of himself when he wrote of them; no need for anything but icy, pitiless transcription. Has it been noticed how inhumanly immoral this great poet is? Not because he drank wine or took drugs. All that has been exaggerated, and, anyway, what does it matter now? But in a much deeper and more deadly sense. It is strange! The world makes such odd blunders. It seems possessed of the idea that absurd amorous scamps like Casanova reach the bottom of wickedness. They do not even approach it. Intrinsically they are quite stupidly "good." Then, again, Byron is supposed to have been a wicked man. He himself aspired to be nothing less. But he was everything less. He was a great, greedy, selfish, swaggering, magnanimous infant! Oscar Wilde is generally regarded as something short of "the just man made perfect," but his simple, babyish passion for touching pretty things, toying with pretty people, wearing pretty clothes, and drinking absinthe, is far too naive a thing to be, at bottom, *evil*. No really wicked person could have written "The Importance of Being Earnest," with those delicious, parodoxical children rallying one another, and "Aunt Augusta" calling aloud for cucumber-sandwiches! Salome itself—that Scarlet Litany —which brings to us, as in a box of alabaster, all the perfumes and odours of amorous lust, is not really a "wicked" play; not wicked, that is to say, unless all mad passion is wicked. Certainly the lust in "Salome" smoulders and glows with a sort of under-furnace of concentration, but, after all, it is the old, universal obsession. Why is it more wicked to say, "Suffer me to kiss thy mouth, Jokanaan!" than to say, "Her lips suck forth my soul— see where it flies!"? Why is it more wicked to say, "Thine eyes are like black holes, burnt by torches in Tyrian tapestry!" than to cry out, as Antony cries out, for the hot kisses of Egypt? Obviously the madness of physical desire is a thing that can hardly be tempered down to the quiet stanzas of Gray's Elegy. But it is not in itself a wicked thing; or the world would never have consecrated it in the great Love-Legends. One may admit that the entrance of the Nubian Executioner changes the situation; but, after all, the frenzy of the girl's request—the terror of that Head upon the silver charger—were implicit in her passion from the beginning; and are, God knows! never very far from passion of that kind.

But all this is changed when we come to Edgar Allen Poe. Here we are no longer in Troy or Antioch or Canopus or Rimini. Here it is not any more a question of ungovernable passion carried to the limit of madness. Here it is no more the human, too human, tradition of each man "killing" the "thing he loves." Here we are in a world where the human element, in passion, has altogether departed, and left something else in its place; something which is really, in the true sense, "inhumanly immoral." In the first place, it is a thing devoid of any physical emotion. It is sterile, immaterial, unearthly, ice-cold. In the second place, it is, in a ghastly sense, self-centered! It feeds upon itself. It subdues everything to itself. Finally, let it be said, it is a thing with a mania for Corruption. The Charnel-House is its bridal-couch, and the midnight stars whisper to one another of its perversion. There is no need for it "to kill the thing it loves," for it loves only what is already dead. *Favete linguis!* There must be no profane misinterpretation of this subtle and delicate difference. In analysing the evasive chemistry of a great poet's mood, one moves warily, reverently, among a thousand betrayals. The mind of such a being is as the sand-strewn floor of a deep sea. In this sea we poor divers for pearls, and *stranger things,* must hold our breath long and long, as we watch the great glittering fish go sailing by, and touch the trailing, rose-coloured weeds, and cross the buried coral. It may be that no one will believe us, when we return, about what we have seen! About those carcanets of rubies round drowned throats and those opals that shimmered and gleamed in dead men's skulls!

At any rate, the most superficial critic of Poe's poetry must admit that every single one of his great verses, except the little one "to Helen," is pre-occupied with Death. Even in that Helen one, perhaps the loveliest, though, I do not think, the most *characteristic,* of all, the poet's desire is to make of the girl he celebrates a sort of Classic Odalisque, round whose palpable contours and lines he may hang the solemn ornaments of the Dead—of the Dead to whom his soul turns, even while embracing the living! Far, far off, from where the real Helen waits, so "statue-like"—the "agate lamp" in her hands—wavers the face of that other Helen, the face "that launched a thousand ships, and burnt the topless towers of Ilium."

The longer poem under the same title, and apparently addressed to the same sorceress, is more entirely "in his mood." Those shadowy, moon-lit "parterres," those living roses— Beardsley has planted them since in another "enchanted garden"—and those "eyes," that grow so luminously, so impossibly large, until it is almost pain to be "saved" by them—these things are in Poe's true manner; for it is not "Helen" that he has ever loved, but her body, her corpse, her ghost, her memory, her sepulchre, her look of dead reproach! And these things none can take from him. The maniacal egoism of a love of this kind—its frozen inhumanity—can be seen even in those poems which stretch yearning hands towards Heaven. In "Annabel Lee," for instance, in that sea-kingdom where the maiden lived who had no thought—who *must* have no thought—"but to love and be loved by me"—what madness of implacable possession, in that "so all the night-tide I lie down by the side of my darling, my darling, my life and my bride, in her sepulchre there by the sea, in her tomb by the sounding sea!"

The same remorseless "laying on of hands" upon what God himself cannot save from us may be discerned in that exquisite little poem which begins:
Thou wast all to me, love,
   For which my soul did pine;
A green isle in the Sea, love,
   A Fountain and a Shrine
All wreathed with Fairy fruits and flowers;
   And all the flowers were mine!
"dim gulf" o'er which the spirit hangs, mute,

EDGAR ALLEN POE

How well, in Poe's world, do we know that motionless, aghast! For still, in those days of his which are "trances," and in those "nightly dreams" which are all he lives for, he is with her; with her still, with her always;
"In what ethereal dances,
By what eternal streams!"
The essence of "immorality" does not lie in mad Byronic passion, or in terrible Herodian lust. It lies in a certain deliberate "petrifaction" of the human soul in us; a certain glacial detachment from all interests save one; a certain frigid insanity of preoccupation with our own emotion. And this emotion, for the sake of which every earthly feeling turns to ice, is our Death-hunger, our eternal craving to make *what has been* be again, and again, forever!

The essence of immorality lies not in the hot flame of natural, or even unnatural, desire. It lies in that inhuman and forbidden wish to arrest *the processes of life*—to lay a freezing hand—a dead hand—upon what we love, so that it *shall always be the same.* The really immoral thing is to isolate, from among the affections and passions and attractions of this human world, one particular lure; and then, having endowed this with the living body of "eternal death," to bend before it, like the satyr before the dead nymph in Aubrey's drawing, and murmur and mutter and shudder over it, through the eternal recurrence of all things!

Is it any longer concealed from us wherein the "immorality" of this lies? It lies in the fact that what we worship, what we *will not,* through eternity, let go, is not a living person, but the "body" of a person; a person who has so far been "drugged," as not only to die for us—that is nothing!—but to remain dead for us, through all the years!

In his own life—with that lovely consumptive Child-bride dying by his side—Edgar Allen Poe lived as "morally," as rigidly, as any Monk. The popular talk about his being a "Drug-Fiend" is ridiculous nonsense. He was a laborious artist, chiselling and refining his "artificial" poems, day in and day out. Where his "immorality" lies is much deeper. It is in the mind—the mind, Master Shallow!—for he is nothing if not an absolute "Celebralist." Certainly Poe's verses are "artificial." They are the most artificial of all poems ever written. And this is natural, because they were the premeditated expression of a premeditated cult. But to say they are artificial does not derogate from their genius. Would that there were more such "artificial" verses in the world!

One wonders if it is clearly understood how the "unearthly" element in Poe differs from the "unearthly" element in Shelley. It differs from it precisely as Death differs from Life.

EDGAR ALLEN POE

Shelley's ethereal spiritualism—though, God knows, such gross animals are we, it seems inhuman enough—is a passionate white flame. It is the thin, wavering fire-point of all our struggles after purity and eternity. It is a centrifugal emotion, not, as was the other's, a centripedal one. It is the noble Platonic rising from the love of one beautiful person to the love of many beautiful persons; and from that onward, through translunar gradations, to the love of the supreme Beauty itself. Shelley's "spirituality" is a living, growing, creative thing. In its intrinsic nature it is not egoistic at all, but profoundly altruistic. It uses Sex to leave Sex behind. In its higher levels it is absolutely Sexless. It may transcend humanity, but it springs from humanity. It is, in fact, humanity's dream of its own transmutation. For all its ethereality and remoteness, it yearns, "like a God in pain," over the sorrows of the world. With infinite planetary pity, it would heal those sorrows.

Edgar Allen's "spirituality" has not the least flicker of a longing to "leave Sex behind." It is bound to Sex, as the insatiable Ghoul is bound to the Corpse he devours. It is not concerned with the physical ecstasies of Sex. It has no interest in such human matters. But deprive it of the fact of Sex-difference, and it drifts away whimpering like a dead leaf, an empty husk, a wisp of chaff, a skeleton gossamer. The poor, actual, warm lips, "so sweetly forsworn," may have had small interest for this "spiritual" lover, but now that she is dead and buried, and a ghost, they must remain a woman's lips forever! Nor have Edgar Allen's "faithful ones" the remotest interest in what goes on around them. Occupied with their Dead, their feeling towards common flesh and blood is the feeling of Caligula. "What have I done to thee?" that proud, reserved face seems to say, as it looks out on us from its dusty title-page; "what have I done to thee, that I should despise thee so?"

Shelley's clear, erotic passion is always a "cosmic" thing. It is the rhythmic expression of the power that creates the world. But there is nothing "cosmic" about the enclosed gardens of Edgar Allen Poe; and the spirits that walk among those Moon-dials and dim Parterres are not of the kind who go streaming up, from land and ocean, shouting with joy that Prometheus has conquered! But what a master he is—what a master! In the suggestiveness of *names*—to mention only one thing—can anyone touch him? That word "Porphyrogene"—the name of the Ruler of, God knows what, Kingdom of the Dead—does it not linger about one—and follow one—like the smell of incense?

But the poem of all poems in which the very genius Edgar Allen is embodied is, of course,

"Ulalume." Like this, there is nothing in Literature—nothing in the whole field of human art. Here he is, from beginning to end, a supreme artist; dealing with the subject for which he was born! That undertone of sardonic, cynical *humour*—for it can be called nothing else—which grins at us in the background like the grin of a Skull; how extraordinarily characteristic it is! And the touches of "infernal colloquialism," so deliberately fitted in, and making us remember—many things!—is there anything in the world like them?

> "And now as the night was senescent,
>   And the star-dials hinted of morn,
> At the end of our path a liquescent
>   And nebulous lustre was born,
> Out of which a miraculous crescent
>   Arose with a duplicate horn—
> Astarte's be-diamonded crescent,
>   Distinct with its duplicate horn!"

"And I said"—but let us pass to his Companion. The cruelty of this conversation with "Psyche" is a thing that may well make us shudder. The implication is, of course, double. Psyche is his own soul; the soul in him which would live, and grow, and change, and know the "Vita Nuova." She is also "the Companion," to whom he has turned for consolation. She is the Second One, the Other One, in whose living caresses he would forget, if it might be, that which lies down there in the darkness!

"Then Psyche, uplifting her finger,
Said, "sadly this star I mistrust,
Its pallor I strangely mistrust.
O hasten! O let us not linger!
O fly! Let us fly! for we must"!"

Thus the Companion; thus the Comrade; thus the "Vita Nuova"!

Now mark what follows:
"Then I pacified Psyche and kissed her,
And tempted her out of her gloom.
And conquered her scruples and gloom.
And we passed to the end of a Vista,
But were stopped by the door of a Tomb.
By the door of a Legended Tomb,
And I said: 'What is written, sweet sister,
On the door of this legended Tomb?'
She replied, Ulalume—Ulalume—
'Tis the vault of thy lost Ulalume!"

The end of the poem is like the beginning, and who can utter the feelings it excites? That "dark tarn of Auber," those "Ghoul-haunted woodlands of Weir" convey, more thrillingly than a thousand words of description, what we have actually felt, long ago, far off, in that strange country of our forbidden dreams.

What a master he is! And if you ask about his "philosophy of life," let the Conqueror Worm make answer:

EDGAR ALLEN POE

"Lo! 'Tis a Gala-Night
Within the lonesome latter years—"
Is not that an arresting commencement? The word "Gala-Night"—has it not the very malice of the truth of things?

Like Heine, it gave this poet pleasure not only to love the Dead, but to love feeling himself dead. That strange poem about "Annie," with its sickeningly sentimental conclusion, where the poet lies prostrate, drugged with all the drowsy syrops in the world, and celebrates his euthanasia, has a quality of its own. It is the "inverse" of life's "Danse Macabre." It is the way we poor dancers long to sleep. "For to sleep you must slumber in just such a bed!" The old madness is over now; the old thirst quenched. It was quenched in a water that "does not flow so far underground." And luxuriously, peacefully, we can rest at last, with the odour of "puritan pansies" about us, and somewhere, not far off, rosemary and rue!

Edgar Allen Poe's philosophy of Life? It may be summed up in the lines from that little poem, where he leaves her side who has, for a moment, turned his heart from the Tomb. The reader will remember the way it begins: "Take this kiss upon thy brow." And the conclusion is the confusion of the whole matter:

"All that we see or seem
Is but a dream within a dream."

Strangely—in forlorn silence—passes before us, as we close his pages, that procession of "dead, cold Maids." Ligeia follows Ulalume; and Lenore follows Ligeia; and after them Eulalie and Annabel; and the moaning of the sea-tides that wash their feet is the moaning of eternity. I suppose it needs a certain kindred perversion, in the reader, to know the shudder of the loss, more dear than life, of such as these! The more normal memory of man will still continue repeating the liturgical syllables of a very different requiem:

> O daughters of dreams and of stories,
> That Life is not wearied of yet—
> Faustine, Fragoletta, Dolores,
> Félise, and Yolande and Julette!

Yes, Life and the Life-Lovers are enamoured still of these exquisite witches, these philtre-bearers, these Sirens, these children of Circe. But a few among us—those who understand the poetry of Edgar Allen—turn away from them, to that rarer, colder, more virginal Figure; to Her who has been born and has died, so many times; to Her who was Ligeia and Ulalume and Helen and Lenore—for are not all these One?—to Her we have loved in vain and shall love in vain until the end—to Her who wears, even in the triumph of her Immortality, the close-clinging, heavily-scented cerements of the Dead!

EDGAR ALLEN POE

"The old bards shall cease and their memory that lingers
Of frail brides and faithless shall be shrivelled as with fire,
For they loved us not nor knew us and our lips were dumb, our fingers
Could wake not the secret of the lyre.
Else, else, O God, the Singer,
I had sung, amid their rages,
The long tale of Man,
And his deeds for good and ill.
But the Old World knoweth—'tis the speech of all his ages—
Man's wrong and ours; he knoweth and is still."

WALT WHITMAN

WALT WHITMAN

I WANT to approach this great Soothsayer from the angle least of all profaned by popular verdicts. I mean from the angle of his poetry. We all know what a splendid heroic Anarchist he was. We all know with what rude zest he gave himself up to that "Cosmic Emotion," to which in these days the world does respectful, if distant, reverence. We know his mania for the word "en masse," for the words "ensemble," "democracy" and "libertad." We know his defiant celebrations of Sex, of amorousness, of maternity; of that Love of Comrades which "passeth the love of women." We know the world-shaking effort he made—and to have made it at all, quite apart from its success, marks him a unique genius!—to write poetry about every mortal thing that exists, and to bring the whole breathing palpable world into his Gargantuan Catalogues. It is absurd to grumble at these Inventories of the Round Earth. They may not all move to Dorian flutes, but they form a background—like the lists of the Kings in the Bible and the lists

of the Ships in Homer—against which, as against the great blank spaces of Life itself, "the writing upon the wall" may make itself visible.

What seems much less universally realized is the extraordinary genius for sheer "poetry" which this Prophet of Optimism possessed. I agree that Walt Whitman's Optimism is the only kind, of that sort of thing, that one can submit to without a blush. At least it is not indecent, bourgeois, and ill-bred, like the fourth-hand Protestantism that Browning dishes up, for the delectation of Ethical Societies. It is the optimism of a person who has seen the American Civil War. It is the optimism of a man who knows "the Bowery," and "the road," and has had queer friends in his mortal pilgrimage.

It is an interesting psychological point, this difference between the "marching breast-forward" of Mrs. Browning's energetic husband, and the "taking to the open road" of Whitman. In some curious way the former gets upon one's nerves where the latter does not. Perhaps it is that the boisterous animal-spirits which one appreciates in the open air become vulgar and irritating when they are practised within the walls of a house. A Satyr who stretches his hairy shanks in the open forest is a pleasant thing to see; but a gentleman, with lavender-colored gloves, putting his feet on the chimney-piece is not so appealing. No doubt it is precisely for these Domestic Exercises that Mr. Chesterton, let us say, would have us love Browning. Well! It is a matter of taste.

But it is not of Walt Whitman's Optimism that I want to speak; it is of his poetry.

To grasp the full importance of what this great man did in this sphere one has only to read modern "libre vers." After Walt Whitman, Paul Fort, for instance, seems simply an eloquent prose writer. And none of them can get the trick of it. None of them! Somewhere, once, I heard a voice that approached it; a voice murmuring of

"Those that sleep upon the wind,
And those that lie along in the rain,
Cursing Egypt—"

But that voice went its way; and for the rest —what banalities! What ineptitudes! They make the mistake, our modern free-versifiers, of thinking that Art can be founded on the Negation of Form. Art can be founded on every other Negation. But not on that one— never on that one! Certainly they have a right to experiment; to invent—if they can— new forms. But they must invent them. They must not just arrange their lines *to look like poetry,* and leave it at that.

Walt Whitman's New Form of Verse was, as all such things must be, as Mr. Hardy's strange poetry, for instance, is, a deliberate and laborious struggle—ending in what is a struggle no more—to express his own personality in a unique and recognisable manner. This is the secret of all "style" in poetry. And it is the absence of this labour, of this premeditated concentration, which leads to the curious result we see on all sides of us, the fact, namely, that all young modern poets *write alike*. They write alike, and they *are* alike—just as all men are like all other men, and all women like all other women, when, without the "art" of clothing, or the "art" of flesh and blood, they lie down side by side in the free cemetery. The old poetic forms will always have their place. They can never grow old-fashioned; any more than Pisanello, or El Greco, or Botticelli, or Scopas, or any ancient Chinese Painter, can grow old-fashioned. But when a modern artist or poet sets to work to create a new form, let him remember what he is doing! It is not the pastime of an hour, this. It is not the casual gesture of a mad iconoclast breaking Classic Statues into mud, out of which to make goblins. It is the fierce, tenacious, patient, constructive work of a lifetime, based upon a tremendous and overpowering Vision! Such a vision Walt Whitman had, and to such constant inspired labour he gave his life—notwithstanding his talk about "loafing and inviting his soul"!

WALT WHITMAN

The "free" poetry of Walt Whitman obeys inflexible, occult laws, the laws commanded unto it by his own creative instinct. We need, as Nietzsche says, to learn the art of "commands" of this kind! Transvaluers of old values do not spend all their time sipping absinthe. Is it a secret still, then, the magical unity of rhythm, which Walt Whitman has conveyed to the words he uses? Those long, plangent, wailing lines, broken by little gurgling gasps and sobs; those sudden thrilling apostrophes and recognitions; those long-drawn flute-notes; those resounding sea-trumpets; all such effects have their place in the great orchestral symphony he conducts!

Take that little poem—quite spoiled before the end by a horrible bit of democratic vulgarity—which begins:
"Come, I will build a Continent indissoluble;
I will make the most splendid race the sun ever shone upon—"
Is it possible to miss the hidden spheric law which governs such a challenge? Take the poem which begins:
"In the growths, by the margins of pond-waters—"
Do you not divine, delicate reader, the peculiar subtlety of that reference to the rank, rain-drenched *anonymous weeds,* which every day we pass in our walks inland? A botanical

name would have driven the magic of it quite away.

Walt Whitman, more than anyone, is able to convey to us that sense of the unclassified pell-mell, of weeds and stones and rubble and wreckage, of vast, desolate spaces, and spaces full of débris and litter, which is most of all characteristic of your melancholy American landscape, but which those who love England know where to find, even among our trim gardens! No one like Walt Whitman can convey to us the magical *ugliness* of certain aspects of Nature—the bleak, stunted, God-forsaken things; the murky pools where the grey leaves fall; the dead reeds where the wind whistles no sweet fairy tunes; the unspeakable margins of murderous floods; the tangled sea-drift, scurfed with scum; the black sea-winrow of broken shells and dead fishes' scales; the roots of willow trees in moonlit places crying out for demon-lovers; the long, moaning grass that grows outside the walls of prisons; the leprous mosses that cover paupers' graves; the mountainous wastes and blighted marshlands which only unknown wild-birds ever touch with their flying wings, and of which madmen dream—these are the things, the ugly, terrible things, that this great optimist turns into poetry. "Yo honk!" cries the wild goose, as it crosses the midnight sky. Others may miss that mad-tossed shadow, that heart-breaking defiance—but from amid the drift of leaves by the roadside, this bearded Fakir of Outcasts has caught its meaning; has heard, and given it its answer.

Ah, gentle and tender reader; thou whose heart, it may be has never cried all night for what it must not name, did you think Swinburne or Byron were the poets of "love"? Perhaps you do not know that the only "short story" on the title-page of which Guy de Maupassant found it in him to write *that word* is a story about the wild things we go out to kill?

Walt Whitman, too, does not confine his notions of love to normal human coquetries. The most devastating love-cry ever uttered, except that of King David over his friend, is the cry this American poet dares to put into the heart of "a wild-bird from Alabama" that has lost its mate. I wonder if critics have done justice to the incredible genius of this man who can find words for that aching of the soul we do not confess even to our dearest? The sudden words he makes use of, in certain connections, awe us, hush us, confound us, take our breath,—as some of Shakespeare's do—with their mysterious congruity. Has my reader ever read the little poem called "Tears"? And what *purity* in the truest, deepest sense, lies behind his pity for such tragic craving; his understanding of what love-stricken, banished ones feel. I do not speak now of his happily amorous verses. They have their place. I speak of those desperate lines that come, here and there, throughout his work, where, with his huge, Titanic back set against the world-wall, and his wild-tossed beard streaming in the wind, he seems *to hold open* by main, gigantic force that door of hope which Fate and God and Man and the Laws of Nature are all endeavoring to close! *And he holds it open!* And it is open still. It is for this reason—let the profane hold their peace!—that I do not hesitate to understand very clearly why he addresses a certain poem to the Lord Christ! Whether it be true or not that the Pure in Heart see God, it is certainly true that they have a power of saving us from God's Law of Cause and Effect! According to this Law, we all "have our reward" and reap what we have sown. But sometimes, like a deep-sea murmur, there rises from the poetry of Walt Whitman a Protest that *must* be heard! Then it is that the Tetrarchs of Science forbid in vain "that one should raise the Dead." For the Dead are raised up, and come forth, even in the likeness wherein we loved them! If words, my friends; if the use of words in poetry can convey such intimations as these to such a generation as ours, can anyone deny that Walt Whitman is a great poet?

WALT WHITMAN

Deny it, who may or will. There will always gather round him—as he predicted—out of City-Tenements and Artist-Studios and Factory-Shops and Ware-Houses and Bordelloes—aye! and, it may be, out of the purlieus of Palaces themselves—a strange, mad, heart-broken company of life-defeated derelicts, who come, not for Cosmic Emotion or Democracy or Anarchy or Amorousness, or even "Comradeship," but for that touch, that whisper, that word, that hand outstretched in the darkness, which makes them *know*—against reason and argument and all evidence—that they may hope still—*for the Impossible is true!*

CONCLUSION

CONCLUSION

E have been together, you who read this—and to you, whoever you are, whether pleased or angry, I make a comrade's signal. Who knows? We might be the very ones to understand each other, if we met! We have been together, in the shadow of the presences that make life tolerable; and now we must draw our conclusion and go our way.

Our conclusion? Ah! that is a hard matter. The world we live in lends itself better to beginnings than conclusions. Or does anything, in this terrible flowing tide, even *begin?* End or beginning, we find ourselves floating upon it—this great tide—and we must do what we can to get a clear glimpse of the high stars before we sink. I wonder if, in the midst of the stammered and blurted incoherences, the lapses and levities, of this quaint book, a sort of "orientation," as the Theologians say now, has emerged at all? I feel, myself, as though it had, though it is hard enough to put it into words. I seem to feel that a point of view, not altogether irrelevant in our time, has projected a certain light upon us, as we advanced together.

Let me try to catch some few filmy threads of this before it vanishes, even though, like a dream in the waking, its outlines waver and recede and fade, until it is lost in space. We gather, then, I fancy, from this kind of hurried passing through enchanted gardens, a sort of curious unwillingness to let our "fixed convictions" deprive us any more of the spiritual adventures to which we have a right. We begin to understand the danger of such convictions, of such opinions, of such "constructive consistency." We grow prepared to "give ourselves up," to "yield ourselves willingly," to whatever new Revelation of the Evasive One chance may throw in our way. It is in such yieldings, such surprises by the road, such new vistas and perspectives, that life loves to embody itself. To refuse them is to turn away from Life and dwell in the kingdom of the shadow.

"Why not?" the Demon who has presided over our wanderings together seems to whisper—"why not for a little while try the experiment of having no "fixed ideas," no "inflexible principles," no "concentrated aim"? Why not simply react to one mysterious visitor after another, as they approach us, and caress or hurt us, and go their way? Why not, for an interlude, be Life's children, instead of her

CONCLUSION

slaves or her masters, and let Her lead us, the great crafty Mother, whither she will?"

There will be much less harm done by such an embracing of Fate, and such a cessation of foolish agitations, than many might suppose. And more than anything else, this is what our generation requires! We are over-ridden by theorists and preachers and ethical water-carriers; we need a little rest—a little yawning and stretching and "being ourselves"; a little quiet sitting at the feet of the Immortal Gods. We need to forget to be troubled, for a brief interval, if the Immortal Gods speak in strange and variable tongues, and offer us diverse-shaped chalices. Let us drink, dear friends, let us drink, as the most noble prophetess Bacbuc used to say! There are many vintages in the kingdom of Beauty; and yet others—God knows! even outside that. Let us drink, and ask no troublesome questions. The modern puritan seeks to change the nature of our natural longing. He tells us that what we need is not less labor but more labor, not less "concentrated effort," but more "concentrated effort"; not "Heaven," in fact, but "Hell."

I do not know. There is much affectation abroad, and some hypocrisy. Puritans were ever addicted to hypocrisy. But because of these "virtuous" prophets of "action," are we to give up our Beatific Vision? Why not be honest for once, and confess that what Man, born of Woman, craves for in his heart is a little joy, a little happiness, a little pleasure, before "he goes hence and is no more seen"? We know that we know nothing. Why, then, pretend that we know the importance of being "up and doing"? There may be no such importance. The common burden of life we have, indeed, all to bear—and they are not very gracious or lovely souls who seek to put it off on others—but for this additional burden, this burden of "being consistent" and having a "strong character," does it seem very wise, in so brief an interval, to put the stress just there?

Somehow I think a constant dwelling in the company of the "great masters" leads us to take with a certain "pinch of salt" the strenuous "duties" which the World's voices make so clamorous! It may be that our sense of their greatness and remoteness produces a certain "humility" in us, and a certain mood of "waiting on the Spirit," not altogether encouraging to what this age, in its fussy worship of energy, calls "our creative work." Well! There is a place doubtless for these energetic people, and their strenuous characters, and their "creative work." But I think there is a place also for those who cannot rush about the market-place, or climb high Alps, or make engines spin, or race, with girded loins, after "Truth." I think there is a place

CONCLUSION

still left for harmless spectators in this Little Theatre of the Universe. And such spectators will do well if they see to it that nothing of the fine or the rare or the exquisite escapes them. Somebody must have the discrimination and the detachment necessary to do justice to our "creative minds." The worst of it is, everybody in these days rushes off to "create," and pauses not a moment to look round to see whether what is being created is worth creating!

We must return to the great masters; we must return to the things in life that really matter; and then we shall acquire, perhaps, in our little way the art of keeping the creators of ugliness at a distance!

Let us at least be honest. The world is a grim game, and we need sometimes the very courage of Lucifer to hold our enemies back. But in the chaos of it all, and the madness and frenzy, let us at least hold fast to that noble daughter of the gods men name *Imagination*. With that to aid us, we can console ourselves for many losses, for many defeats. For the life of the Imagination flows deep and swift, and in its flowing it can bear us to undreamed-of coasts, where the children of fantasy and the children of irony dance on—heedless of theory and argument.

The world is deep, as Zarathustra says, and deep is pain; and deeper than pain is joy. I do not think that they have reached the final clue, even with their talk of "experience" and "struggle," and the "storming of the heights." Sometimes it is not from "experience," but from beyond experience, that the rumour comes. Sometimes it is not from the "struggle," but from the "rest" after the struggle, that the whisper is given. Sometimes the voice comes to us, not from the "heights," but from the depths.

The truth seems to be that if the clue is to be caught at all, it will be caught where we least expect it; and, for the catching of it, what we have to do is not to let our theories, our principles, our convictions, our opinions, impede our vision—but now and then to lay them aside; but whether with them or without them, to be *prepared*—for the Spirit bloweth where it listeth and we cannot tell whence it cometh, or whither it goeth!

ERRATA

For Edgar Allen Poe read Edgar Allan Poe.

Page 33, line 1, for "and goose-girls. These are the things" read "and goose-girls—these are the things."

Page 33, line 19, for "Penetre" read "Peut-etre."

Page 50, line 10, for "iron" read "urn."

Page 59, line 16, for "De Vinci" read "Da Vinci."

Page 129, line 8, for "Berwick" read "Bewick."

Page 138, line 25, for "Cabbalistic" read "Cabalistic."

Pages 268/269, line 30, and line 1, for "dim-gulf," etc., read

"That dim-gulf o'er which
  The spirit lies, mute, motionless, aghast—
how well, in Poe's world, we know that! For still, in those days," etc.

Page 270, line 20, for Celebralist read Cerebralist.

Page 285, line 12, for "long-drawn" read "far-drawn."

THE LIBRARY
ST. MARY'S COLLEGE OF MARYLAND
ST. MARY'S CITY, MARYLAND 20686